OFF
CENTER
Patchwork

Cheryl A. Adam

American Quilter's Society

P. O. Box 3290 • Paducah, KY 42002-3290

www.AQSquilt.com

Located in Paducah, Kentucky, the American Quilter's Society (AQS) is dedicated to promoting the accomplishments of today's quilters. Through its publications and events, AQS strives to honor today's quiltmakers and their work and to inspire future creativity and innovation in quiltmaking.

EDITOR: JANE TOWNSWICK
GRAPHIC DESIGN: ANGELA SCHADE
COVER DESIGN: MICHAEL BUCKINGHAM
PHOTOGRAPHY: CHARLES R. LYNCH

Library of Congress Cataloging-in-Publication Data
Adam, Cheryl A.
　　　Off center patchwork / Cheryl A. Adam
　　　　　　　　　　　p.　　　　cm.
　　　ISBN 1-57432-802-6
　　　1. Patchwork--Patterns.　　2. Patchwork--Quilts.
I. Title.
TT835 .A315　2002
746.46'041--dc21　　　　　　　　　　　　　　　　　2002151002
　　　　　　　　　　　　　　　　　　　　　　　　　　　　　CIP

Additional copies of this book may be ordered from the American Quilter's Society, PO Box 3290, Paducah, KY 42002-3290, or online at www.AQSquilt.com.

DEDICATION

There are many people to whom I wish to dedicate this book. First and foremost is my family: my husband, Bob; my sons, Martin and Jeff; and my parents, who have always encouraged me to try new ideas and are my biggest cheerleaders. Then, there are the friends who helped make this book possible by giving up their valuable time to make samples. Finally, my many quilting friends who have always showed interest in my work. Thanks!

HOW TO USE THIS BOOK

The patterns in this book are arranged in order of blocks that have the least number of pieces to those that feature the greatest number of pieces. Look through the projects on the following pages carefully, and choose a pattern that interests you. Take a few minutes to study the color photo of that quilt, noting where color, contrast, and value changes enhance the design, then use that knowledge to help select the colors for your own quilt. If you are feeling unsure about your fabric choices, photocopy the off-center version of the block several times and color in some mock-up blocks to explore various color combinations. When you come up with a color scheme that pleases you, you'll be ready to start making your quilt.

If you'd like to start experimenting with block placements in addition to color, make multiple photocopies of an off-center block that interests you, and color in the photocopies in different ways. Then play with block placements, and take time to evaluate each new layout you try. You'll enjoy a sense of achievement that comes from making quilts that are unique expressions of your own creativity.

CONTENTS

INTRODUCTION

Several years ago I read an article about making an offset Pineapple block. I thought it was an interesting idea and tried it. The quilt was stunning. By putting the center of the block off to one corner, the block had a more graphic and contemporary look. It just seemed to beg for a different way of coloring, using many different fabrics, and grouping them on two adjoining sides instead of the traditional opposite sides. With this simple drafting change, I was able to go from a very traditional design to a dynamic, contemporary quilt. This was the start of my experiments.

Next, I tried working with a Kaleidoscope block. I was never very excited about this traditional design, but when I redrafted it off-center, it became very interesting. Using the altered version of the block, I was able to make a quilt that created the effect of looking through a real kaleidoscope, and it was easy to accomplish without any complex fabric-cutting techniques or difficult piecing. My quilter friends were amazed by the way I had done this, and they encouraged me to develop this technique further.

I began looking through my quilt books for other traditional blocks that could be redone with my off-center drafting methods and continued making more and more patterns this way. I chose quilt designs that featured the simple Nine-Patch block, as well as more difficult ones such as Bear's Paw and Double Dutch. Each time I set blocks off-center, I was surprised at how different the resulting quilts looked from their traditional counterparts. I was even more pleased when I found out that, like the traditional designs, the new blocks were easy to arrange in many ways to create brand new quilt designs.

As you look through the following pages, you will notice that many of the quilts have a traditional look when made in traditional colors and fabrics. However, they can also look contemporary when done in the bright, unconventional fabrics on the market today.

As you make these quilts, have fun! Experiment, and use colors you've never dared use with a traditional pattern. The line diagrams at the back of the book will enable you to experiment with color and cut-and-paste your own unique quilt designs with off-center blocks. You will find, as I did, that the design possibilities are endless and that these blocks will keep you in new quilt ideas for a long time!

Cheryl A. Adam

46" x 58"

The off-center Nine-Patch blocks have been rotated by a quarter-turn three times and sewn together to make a large plaid block. Twelve of these larger blocks create the quilt center.   Made by Helen McCalla, Bloomington, Illinois.

NINE-PATCH

Finished blocks: 6" square

Fabrics and Supplies

Navy	½ yard
Blue print	¾ yard
Cream	¾ yard
Burgundy	⅜ yard
Cream print	⅛ yard
Navy inner border	¼ yard
Blue print outer border	¾ yard
Backing	3⅝ yards
Batting	50" x 62"
Binding	½ yard

Cutting List

Note: Cut all strips across the 42" fabric width.

For Nine-Patch Blocks

Fabric	Quantity	Strip width
Navy	4 strips	1½"
	2 strips	3½"
Blue print	4 strips	2½"
	3 strips	3½"
Cream	4 strips	3½"
	3 strips	2½"
Burgundy	3 strips	1½"
	2 strips	2½"
Cream print	2 strips	1½"

For Borders, Backing, and Binding

Navy inner border	5 strips	1½"
Blue print outer border	5 strips	4½"
Backing	2 strips	42" x 62"
Binding	6 strips	desired width

Off-set Nine-Patch block

Traditional Nine-Patch block

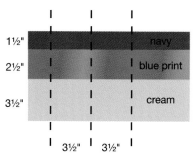

1½" navy
2½" blue print
3½" cream

3½"   3½"

Cut 48

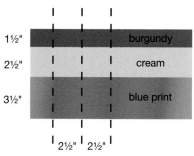

1½" burgundy
2½" cream
3½" blue print

2½"   2½"

Cut 48

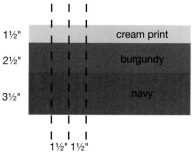

1½" cream print
2½" burgundy
3½" navy

1½" 1½"

Cut 48

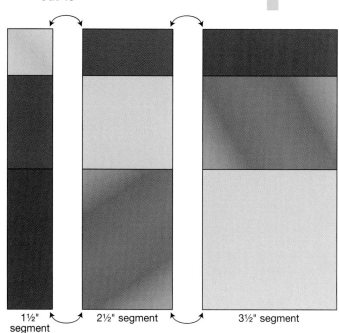

1½"
segment

2½" segment

3½" segment

Block assembly

Piecing the Nine-Patch Blocks

1. Sew a 1½"-wide navy strip, a 2½"-wide blue print strip, and a 3½"-wide cream strip into a strip-set. Press. Repeat with the remaining navy, blue print, and cream strips. Cut the strip-sets into 48 segments, each 3½" wide.

2. Sew a 1½"-wide burgundy strip, a 2½"-wide cream strip, and a 3½"-wide blue print strip into a strip-set. Press. Repeat with remaining burgundy, cream, and blue print strips and cut the strip-sets into 48 segments, each 2½" wide.

3. Sew a 1½"-wide cream print strip, a 2½"-wide burgundy strip, and a 3½"-wide navy strip into a strip-set. Press. Repeat with remaining cream print, burgundy, and navy strips, and cut the strip-sets into 48 segments, each 1½" wide.

4. Sew the segments from steps 1 through 3 together to create a Nine-Patch block. Make 48 of these blocks.

Assembling the Quilt Center

1. Referring to the quilt assembly diagram, sew the blocks together in eight rows of six blocks each. Press.

2. Sew the rows of blocks together. Press the completed quilt center.

Adding the Borders

1. Referring to the quilt assembly diagram, sew a 1½"-wide navy border strip to the top and one to the bottom of the quilt center. Press. Trim the excess fabric even with the edges of the quilt center.

2. Cut a 1½"-wide navy strip in half. Sew each half-strip to a full 1½"-wide navy strip to make two side inner border strips.

3. Sew the two side inner border strips to the sides of the quilt. Press. Trim the excess fabric even with the edges of the quilt.

4. Sew two of the 4½"-wide blue print strips to the top and bottom of the quilt center. Press. Trim the excess fabric even with the edges of the quilt center.

5. Cut one of the remaining 4½" blue print strips in half. Sew each half-strip to a full 4½"-wide blue print strip to make a side outer border strip.

6. Sew the two side outer border strips to the sides of the quilt center. Press. Trim the excess fabric even with the edges of the quilt.

Finishing

1. Sew the two backing strips together and press the seam allowance open.

2. Layer the backing, batting, and quilt top. Quilt by hand or machine, as desired.

3. Sew the binding strips together to form one long strip. Fold the binding in half lengthwise, with wrong sides together, and press. Sew the raw edges of the binding to the edges of the front of the quilt. Turn the folded edge of the binding to the back of the quilt and stitch in place by hand, mitering the corner seams.

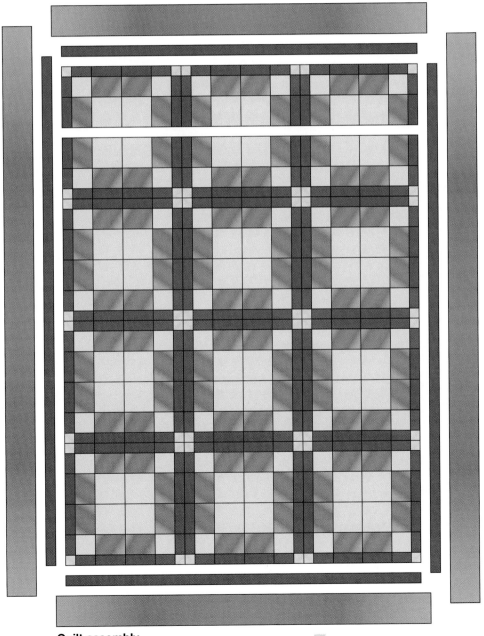

Quilt assembly

86" x 86"

These Rail Fence blocks feature all the same colors, but every other block is rotated by a quarter-turn to create the zigzag pattern throughout the quilt.

Made by Anne Powell, Normal, Illinois.

RAIL FENCE

Finished blocks: 12" square

Fabrics and Supplies

Blue print	1⅜ yards
Beige print	1⅜ yards
Multi-color print	1⅜ yards
Red	1 yard
Red print	¾ yard
Red inner border	¾ yard
Multi-color print outer border	1½ yards
Backing	7⅞ yards
Batting	90" x 90"
Binding	1 yard

Cutting List

Note: Cut all strips across the 42" fabric width.

For Rail Fence Blocks

Fabric	Quantity	Strip width
Blue print	12 strips	3½"
Beige print	12 strips	3½"
Multi-color print	12 strips	3½"
Red	21 strips	1½"
Red print	15 strips	1½"

For Borders, Backing, and Binding

Red inner border	8 strips	2½"
Multi-color print outer border	9 strips	5½"
Backing	3 strips	30" x 90"
Binding	9 strips	desired width

Piecing the Rail Fence Blocks

1. Sew a 3½"-wide multi-color print strip, a 3½"-wide blue strip, and a 3½"-wide beige strip into a strip-set. Press. Repeat with the remaining 3½" blue, beige, and multi-color print strips for a total of 12 strip-sets. From these sets, cut 36 segments, each 9½" wide, and 36 segments, each 3½" wide. The segments from the first strip-set should measure 9½" square. The segments from the second strip-set should measure 3½" x 9½".

2. Sew 1½"-wide red strips to both sides of a 1½"-wide red print strip. Press. Make nine of these strip-sets. From these sets, cut 36 segments, each 9½" wide.

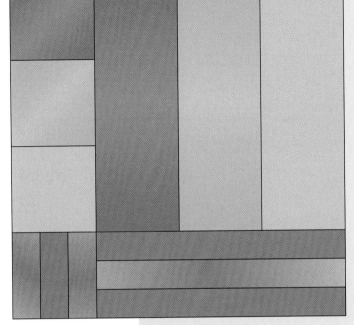

Off-set Rail Fence block

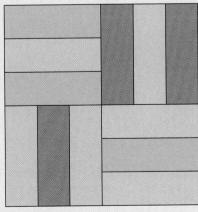

Traditional Rail Fence block

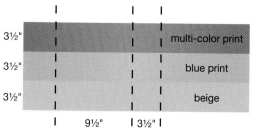

3½" — multi-color print

3½" — blue print

3½" — beige

9½"   3½"

Cut 36 of both segment widths

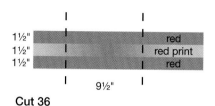

1½" — red
1½" — red print
1½" — red

9½"

Cut 36

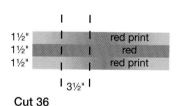

1½" — red print
1½" — red
1½" — red print

3½"

Cut 36

Block assembly

3. Sew 1½"-wide red print strips to both sides of a 1½"-wide red strip. Press. Make three of these strip-sets. From these sets, cut 36 segments, each 3½" wide.

4. Assemble the segments in two rows, as shown in the block assembly diagram and press. Sew the rows together and press. Make 36 Rail Fence blocks.

Assembling the Quilt Center

1. Referring to the quilt assembly diagram, sew the blocks together in six rows of six blocks each. Press.

2. Sew the rows of blocks together and press.

Adding the Borders

1. Sew the 2½"-wide red strips together in pairs to make four inner border strips.

2. Referring to the quilt assembly diagram, sew inner border strips to the top and bottom of the quilt center. Press. Trim the excess fabric even with the edges of the quilt center.

3. Sew the remaining inner border strips to the sides of the quilt center. Press. Trim the excess fabric even with the edges of the quilt center.

4. Sew eight of the 5½"-wide multi-color print strips together in pairs to make four outer border strips. Cut the remaining 5½" strip in half. Sew one half-strip to the end of one long border strip, and the second half-strip to another long strip.

5. Sew the two shorter outer border strips to the top and bottom of the quilt center. Press. Trim the excess fabric even with the edges of the quilt center.

6. Sew the longer border strips to the sides of the quilt center. Press. Trim the excess fabric even with the edges of the quilt.

Finishing

1. Sew the three backing strips together and press the seam allowances open.

2. Layer the backing, batting, and quilt top. Quilt by hand or machine, as desired.

3. Sew the binding strips together to form one long strip. Fold the binding in half lengthwise, with wrong sides together, and press. Sew the raw edges of the binding to the edges of the front of the quilt. Turn the folded edge of the binding to the back of the quilt and stitch in place by hand, mitering the corner seams.

Quilt assembly

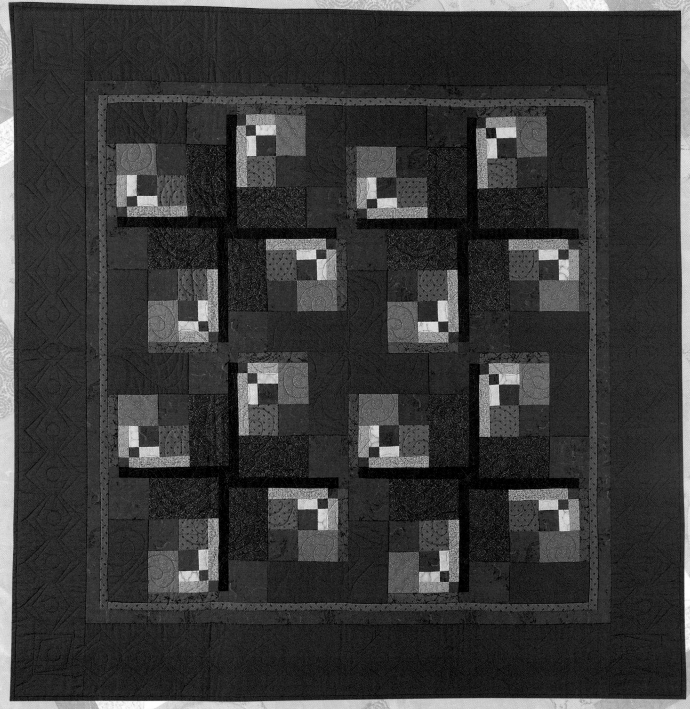

65" x 65"

Four Log Cabin with a Chain blocks have been rotated by a quarter-turn and sewn together to make a larger block. Four of the larger blocks are used to create the quilt center.

Made by Nancy Simms, Cooksville, Illinois.

LOG CABIN WITH A CHAIN

Finished blocks: 12" square

Fabrics and Supplies

Red	(R)	¾ yard
Green 1	(G-1)	⅛ yard
Green 2	(G-2)	¼ yard
Green 3	(G-3)	¼ yard
Green 4	(G-4)	⅝ yard
Green 5	(G-5)	½ yard
Purple 1	(P-1)	⅛ yard
Purple 2	(P-2)	⅛ yard
Purple 3	(P-3)	⅜ yard
Purple 4	(P-4)	¼ yard
Purple 5	(P-5)	⅝ yard
G-2 inner border		¼ yard
Red middle border		⅜ yard
P-5 outer border		1¼ yards
Backing		4 yards
Batting		69" x 69"
Binding		¾ yard

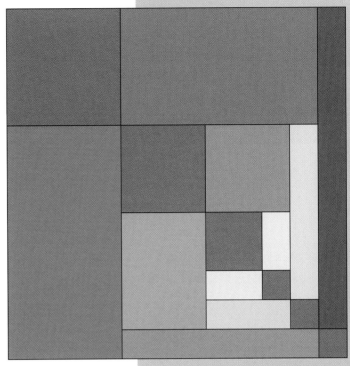

Off-set Log Cabin with a Chain block

Cutting List

Note: Cut all strips across the 42" fabric width.

For Log Cabin with a Chain Blocks

Fabric	Quantity	Strip width	Pieces to cut from strips
R	1 strip	2½"	
	3 strips	1½"	
	2 strips	3½"	
	2 strips	4½"	
G-1	1 strip	2½"	
G-2	2 strips	3½"	16 squares, 3½" x 3½"
G-3	1 strip	6½"	
G-4	4 strips	4½"	16 rectangles, 4½" x 7½"
G-5	1 strip	11½"	
P-1	1 strip	1½"	
P-2	2 strips	1½"	16 rectangles, 1½" x 3½"
P-3	2 strips	4½"	
P-4	4 strips	1½"	16 rectangles, 1½" x 7½"
P-5	2 strips	8½"	

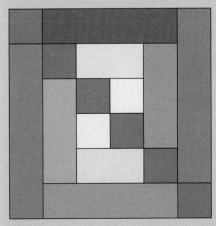

Traditional Log Cabin with a Chain block

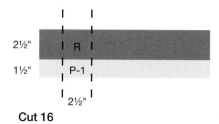

2½"
1½"

R
P-1

2½"

Cut 16

2½"
1½"

G-1
R

1½"

Cut 16

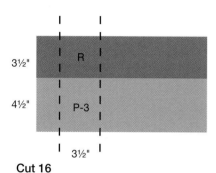

3½"

4½"

R

P-3

3½"

Cut 16

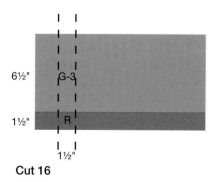

6½"

1½"

G-3

R

1½"

Cut 16

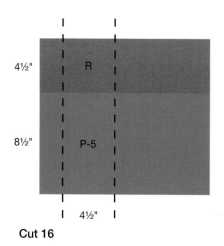

4½"

8½"

R

P-5

4½"

Cut 16

For Borders, Backing, and Binding

Fabric	Quantity	Strip width
G-2 inner border	5 strips	1½"
Red middle border	5 strips	2"
P-5 outer border	6 strips	6½"
Backing	2 strips	35" x 69"
Binding	7 strips	desired width

Piecing the Log Cabin with a Chain Blocks

1. Referring to the cutting diagrams, sew the following strip-sets and cut into segments:

> 2½"-wide R and 1½"-wide P-1; make 1 strip-set;
> cut 16 – 2½" segments.
> 2½"-wide G-1 and 1½"-wide R; make 1 strip-set;
> cut 16 – 1½" segments.
> 3½"-wide R and 4½"-wide P-3; make 2 strip-sets;
> cut 16 – 3½" segments.
> 6½"-wide G-3 and 1½"-wide R; make 1 strip-set;
> cut 16 – 1½" segments.
> 4½"-wide R and 8½"-wide P-5; make 2 strip-sets;
> cut 16 – 4½" segments.
> 11½"-wide G-5 and 1½"-wide R; make 1 strip-set;
> cut 16 – 1½" segments.

2. Following unit construction diagrams, sew segments and cut pieces in the following order to make each block. Make a total of 16 blocks.

> **Unit A.** Sew an R/P-1 segment to a G-1/R segment.
> **Unit B.** Sew a P-2 (1½" x 3½") rectangle to bottom of unit A.
> **Unit C.** Sew a G-2 (3½" x 3½") square to top of unit B.
> **Unit D.** Sew a R/P-3 segment to left side of unit C.
> **Unit E.** Sew a G-3/R segment to right side of unit D.
> **Unit F.** Sew a P-4 (1½" x 7½") rectangle to bottom of unit E.
> **Unit G.** Sew a G-4 (4½" x 7½") rectangle to top of unit F.
> **Unit H.** Sew an R/P-5 segment to left side of unit G.
> **Unit I.** Sew a G-5/R segment to right side of unit H.

Assembling the Quilt Center

1. Referring to the quilt assembly diagram, sew the blocks together in four rows of four blocks each. Press.

2. Sew the rows of blocks together and press.

Adding the Borders

1. Cut one of the 1½"-wide G-2 inner border strips into four equal pieces. Sew one of these pieces to each of the remaining full-length G-2 inner border strips.

2. Referring to the quilt assembly diagram, sew two of the inner border strips to the top and bottom of the quilt center. Press. Trim the excess fabric even with the edges of the quilt center.

3. Sew the remaining two inner border strips to the sides of the quilt center. Press. Trim the excess fabric even with the edges of the quilt center.

4. Cut one of the 2"-wide red middle border strips into four equal pieces. Sew one of these pieces to each of the remaining full-length red middle border strips.

5. Sew two of the middle border strips to the top and bottom of the quilt center. Press. Trim the excess fabric even with the edges of the quilt center.

6. Sew the remaining two middle border strips to the sides of the quilt center. Press. Trim the excess fabric even with the edges of the quilt center.

7. Cut two of the 4¾"-wide P-5 outer border strips in half. Sew one of these pieces to each of the remaining full-length P-5 outer border strips.

8. Sew two of the outer border strips to the top and bottom of the quilt center. Press. Trim the excess fabric even with the edges of the quilt center.

9. Sew the remaining two outer border strips to the sides of the quilt. Press. Trim the excess fabric even with the edges of the quilt.

Finishing

1. Sew the two backing strips together and press the seam allowance open.

2. Layer the backing, batting, and quilt top. Quilt by hand or machine, as desired.

3. Sew the binding strips together to form one long strip. Fold the binding in half lengthwise, with wrong sides together, and press. Sew the raw edges of the binding to the edges of the front of the quilt. Turn the folded edge of the binding to the back of the quilt and stitch in place by hand, mitering the corner seams.

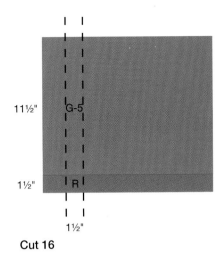

11½" G-5
1½" R
1½"

Cut 16

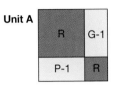

Unit A
R   G-1
P-1   R

Unit B
P-2

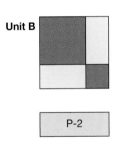

Unit C
G-2

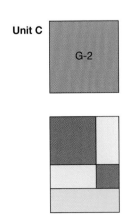

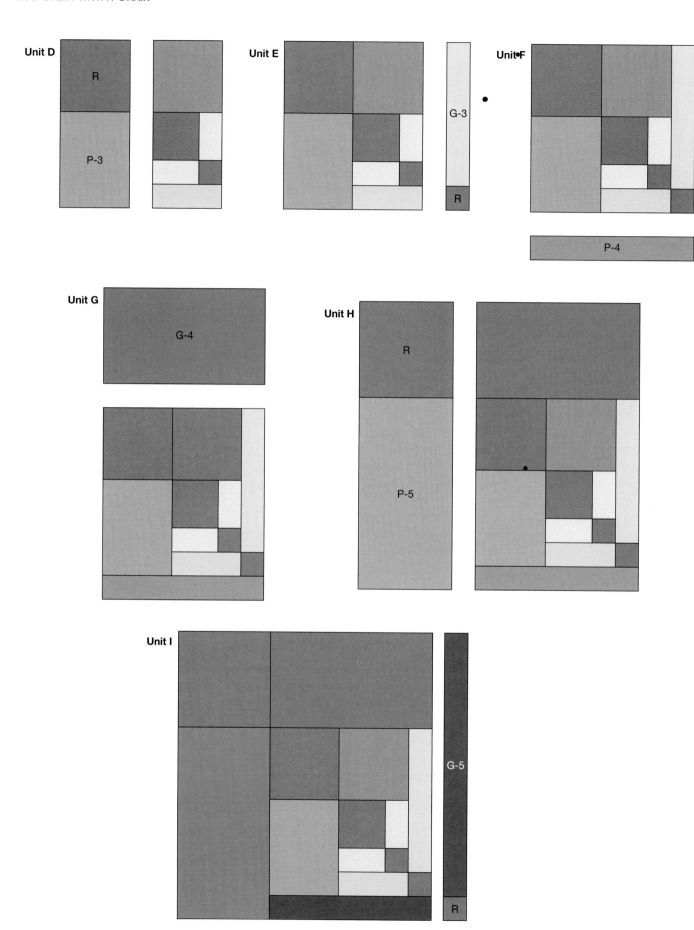

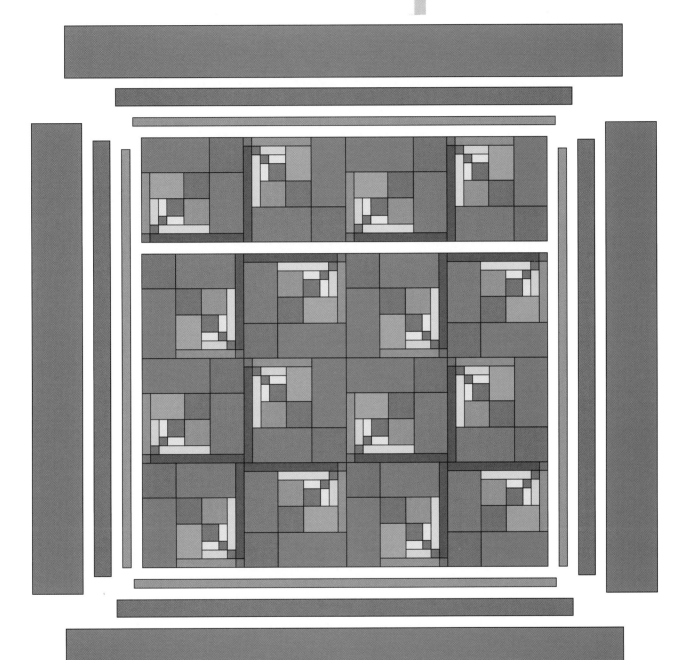

Quilt assembly

26" x 26"

The center of the Pinwheel block is moved toward a corner, then the block is redrafted to create a more contemporary version of this traditional favorite block. The blocks are paper-pieced with all the pinwheels placed in the same direction in the quilt center.

Made by the author.

PINWHEEL

Finished blocks: 6" square

Fabrics and Supplies

Red-gray print	½ yard
Gray	⅜ yard
Coral	⅝ yard
Gray inner border	⅛ yard
Red-gray outer border	⅜ yard
Backing	1 yard
Batting	30" x 30"
Binding	⅜ yard

Cutting List

Note: Fabric for paper piecing must be cut at least ½" larger than the patterns on all sides. Patterns are on page 23.

For Pinwheel Blocks

Fabric	Quantity	Pieces
Red-gray print	9	Section A-1
	9	Section A-5
	9	Section B-1
	9	Section B-5
Gray	9	Section A-3
	9	Section A-7
	9	Section B-3
	9	Section B-7
Coral	9	Section A-2
	9	Section A-4
	9	Section A-6
	9	Section A-8
	9	Section B-2
	9	Section B-4
	9	Section B-6
	9	Section B-8

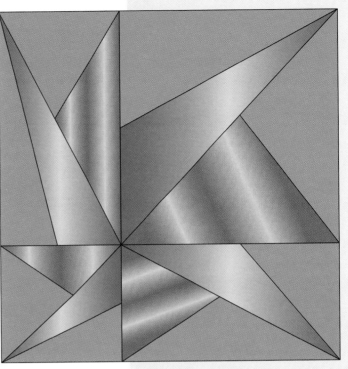

Off-set Pinwheel block

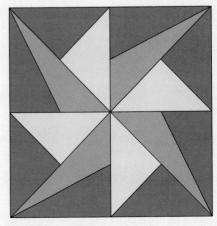

Traditional Pinwheel block

For Borders, Backing, and Binding

Note: Cut all strips across the 42" fabric width.

Gray inner border	2 strips	Cut into two 1½" x 18½" and two 1½" x 20½" pieces
Red-gray outer border	3 strips	Cut into two 3½" x 20½" and two 3½" x 26½" pieces
Backing	1 square	30" x 30"
Binding	3 strips	desired width

Paper-Piecing the Pinwheel Blocks

1. Photocopy the paper-piecing patterns onto lightweight paper. You will need nine copies of each section of the Pinwheel block.

2. Cut the fabrics listed for the pattern sections. Remember to do this from the unmarked side of the paper and with the right side of the fabrics facing up.

3. Place piece A-1 on the unmarked side of the Pinwheel pattern, right side up, making sure that it covers the entire area of the pattern piece. Place piece A-2, right side up, positioning it so it covers its pattern piece. Carefully flip piece A-2 over onto piece A-1 so that the right sides are together, making sure that fabric from both pieces is positioned on the sewing lines, to allow for the seam allowances. Pin the pieces in place on the pattern. Turn the pattern over, and stitch on the line between pieces A-1 and A-2.

4. Flip piece A-2 open, so that the right side of the fabric is facing up, and press. Check to make sure that the fabrics cover the entire pattern pieces.

5. Repeat steps 3 and 4 for each of the remaining pattern pieces in sections A and B. After completing both sections, sew them together as indicated on the patterns to complete the Pinwheel block. Make a total of nine Pinwheel blocks.

6. Trim the outside seam allowances of each Pinwheel block to ¼" and carefully tear off the paper.

Assembling the Quilt Center

1. Referring to the quilt assembly diagram, sew the Pinwheel blocks together in three rows of three blocks each. Press.

2. Sew the rows of blocks together and press.

Adding the Borders

1. Referring to the quilt assembly diagram, sew the two 1½" x 18½" gray inner border strips to the top and bottom of the quilt center. Press.

2. Sew the two 1½" x 20½" gray inner border strips to the sides of the quilt center. Press.

3. Sew the two 3½" x 20½" red-gray outer border strips to the top and bottom of the quilt center. Press.

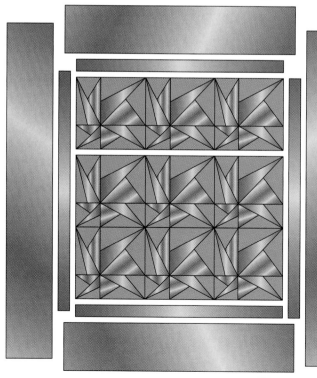

Quilt assembly

4. Sew the two 3½" x 26½" red-gray outer border strips to the sides of the quilt. Press.

Finishing

1. Layer the backing, batting, and quilt top. Quilt by hand or machine, as desired.

2. Sew the binding strips together to form one long strip. Fold the binding in half lengthwise, with wrong sides together, and press. Sew the raw edges of the binding to the edges of the front of the quilt. Turn the folded edge of the binding to the back of the quilt and stitch in place by hand, mitering the corner seams.

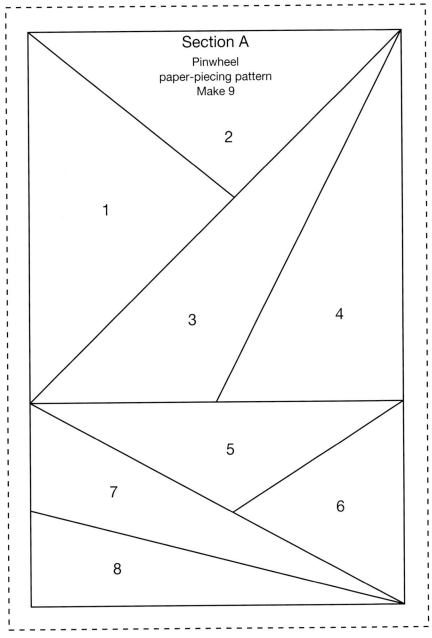

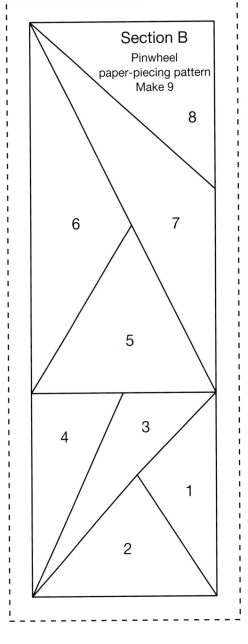

Solid lines are seam lines

84" x 84"

One half of the Churn Dash blocks in this quilt are pieced in one arrangement of colors, and the other half feature a different color placement. The two blocks are then alternated in the quilt center, with every other row turned upside down.

Made by Cindy Walter, Bloomington, Illinois.

CHURN DASH

Finished blocks: 12" square

Fabrics

Gold	1 yard
Blue	2¾ yards
Multi-color print	1¾ yard
Red	1 yard
Gold inner border	¾ yard
Blue outer border	1⅛ yards
Backing	7⅞ yards
Batting	88" x 88"
Binding	1 yard

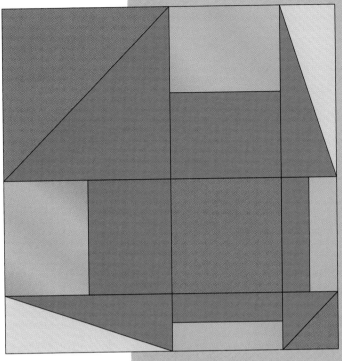

Off-set Churn Dash block

Cutting List

Note: Cut all strips across the 42" fabric width.
Pattern pieces A and Ar are on page 28.

For Churn Dash Blocks

Fabric	Quantity	Strip width	Pieces to cut from strips
Gold	4 strips	2⅝"	18 A triangles and 18 Ar triangles
	4 strips	1½" for E	
	4 strips	3½" for C	
Blue	3 strips	6⅞"	18 B squares, each 6⅞" x 6⅞"
	2 strips	2⅞"	18 F squares, each 2⅞" x 2⅞"
	8 strips	2⅝"	36 A triangles and 36 Ar triangles
	8 strips	1½" for E	
	8 strips	3½" for C	
Multi-color print	4 strips	2⅝"	18 A triangles and 18 Ar triangles
	2 strips	6⅞"	9 B squares, each 6⅞" x 6⅞"
	1 strip	2⅞"	9 F squares, each 2⅞" x 2⅞"
	2 strips	4½"	18 D squares, each 4½" x 4½"
	4 strips	1½" for E	
	4 strips	3½" for C	

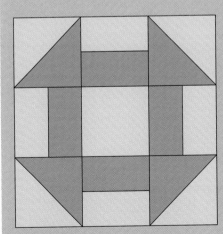

Traditional Churn Dash block

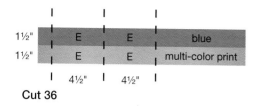

1½"   E   E   blue
1½"   E   E   multi-color print
4½"   4½"

Cut 36

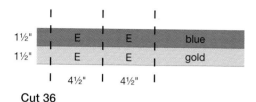

1½"   E   E   blue
1½"   E   E   gold
4½"   4½"

Cut 36

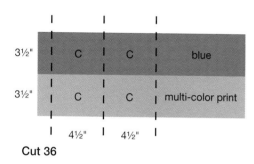

3½"   C   C   blue
3½"   C   C   multi-color print
4½"   4½"

Cut 36

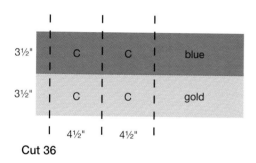

3½"   C   C   blue
3½"   C   C   gold
4½"   4½"

Cut 36

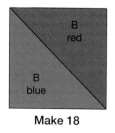

B red / B blue

Make 18

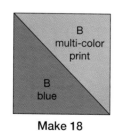

B multi-color print / B blue

Make 18

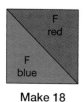

F red / F blue

Make 18

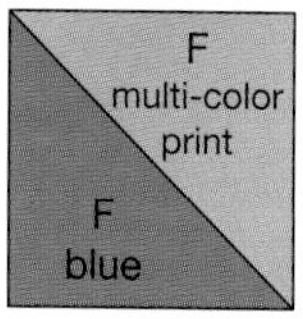

F multi-color print / F blue

Make 18

Fabric	Quantity	Strip width	Pieces to cut from strips
Red	2 strips	6⅞"	9 B squares, each 6⅞" x 6⅞"
	1 strip	2⅞"	9 F squares, each 2⅞" x 2⅞"
	2 strips	4½"	18 D squares, each 4½" x 4½"

For Borders, Backing, and Binding

Gold inner border	8 strips	2½"
Blue outer border	8 strips	4½"
Backing	3 strips	30" x 90"
Binding	9	desired width

Piecing the Churn Dash Blocks

1. Sew a 1½"-wide blue strip and a 1½"-wide multi-color strip into a strip-set. Press. Make four strip-sets in this color combination. Cut the strip-sets into 36 segments, each 4½" wide.

2. Repeat Step 1 with the 1½"-wide blue and gold strips. Cut 36 segments in this color combination, each 4½" wide.

3. Sew a 3½" blue strip and a 3½" multi-color strip into a strip-set. Press. Make four strip-sets in this color combination. Cut the strip-sets into 36 segments, each 4½" wide.

4. Repeat Step 3 with the 3½"-wide blue and gold strips. Cut 36 segments in this color combination, each 4½" wide.

5. With a fabric pencil, mark a diagonal line on the wrong side of the blue 6⅞" B squares. With right sides together, place a blue square on a 6⅞" red B square, matching the edges. Sew a ¼" seam on each side of the marked diagonal line. Cut along the diagonal line, creating two half-square triangle units. Press. Repeat eight times for 18 half-square triangle units in this color combination.

6. Repeat Step 5 with nine blue and nine multi-color 6⅞" B squares. Make 18 half-square triangle units in this color combination. Press.

7. With a fabric pencil, mark a diagonal on the wrong side of the blue 2⅞" F squares. With right sides together, place a blue 2⅞" F square on a red 2⅞" F square. Sew a ¼" seam on each side of the marked diagonal line. Cut along the diagonal line, creating two half-square triangle units. Press. Repeat eight times for 18 half-square triangle units in this color combination.

8. Repeat Step 7 with nine blue and nine multi-color 2⅞" F squares. Make 18 half-square triangle units in this color combination. Press.

OFF CENTER PATCHWORK   Cheryl A. Adam

9. With right sides together, sew the long edge of a blue A triangle to the long edge of a gold A triangle. Press. Make 18 A/A units in this color combination.

10. Repeat Step 9 with 18 blue A triangles and 18 multi-color A triangles.

11. With right sides together, sew the long edge of a blue Ar triangle to the long edge of a gold Ar triangle. Press. Make 18 Ar/Ar units in this color combination.

12. Repeat Step 11 with 18 blue Ar triangles and 18 multi-color Ar triangles.

13. Referring to the block assembly diagram, sew the Churn Dash blocks together in three horizontal rows. Press. Sew the three rows together to complete each block. Press. Make 18 Churn Dash blocks in color combination #1 and 18 blocks in color combination #2 (see page 28).

Assembling the Quilt Center

1. Referring to the quilt assembly diagram, sew the blocks together in six rows of six blocks each. Press.

2. Sew the rows of blocks together and press.

Adding the Borders

1. Sew the 2½"-wide gold inner border strips together in pairs to make four strips. Press.

2. Referring to the quilt assembly diagram, sew two inner border strips to the top and bottom of the quilt center. Press. Trim the excess fabric even with the edges of the quilt center.

3. Sew the remaining 2½"-wide inner border strips to the two sides of the quilt center. Press. Trim the excess fabric even with the edges of the quilt center.

4. Sew the 4½"-wide blue outer border strips together in pairs to make four strips. Press.

5. Sew two outer border strips to the top and bottom of the quilt center. Press. Trim the excess fabric even with the edges of the quilt center.

6. Sew the remaining two outer border strips to the sides of the quilt center. Press. Trim the excess fabric even with the edges of the quilt.

A gold / A blue

A multi-color print / A blue

Make 18   Make 18

Ar gold / Ar blue

Make 18

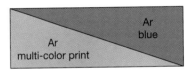
Ar multi-color print / Ar blue

Make 18

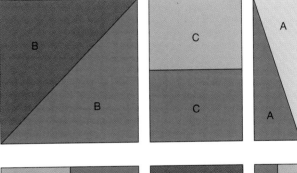
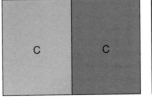

Block assembly

Finishing

1. Sew the three backing strips together and press the seam allowance open.

2. Layer the backing, batting, and quilt top. Quilt by hand or machine, as desired.

3. Sew the binding strips together to form one long strip. Fold the binding in half lengthwise, with wrong sides together, and press. Sew the raw edges of the binding to the edges of the front of the quilt. Turn the folded edge of the binding to the back of the quilt and stitch in place by hand, mitering the corner seams.

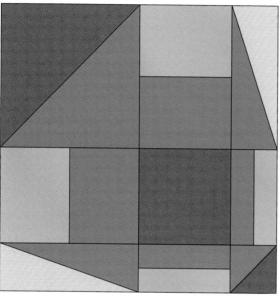

Churn Dash block color combination 1; make 18

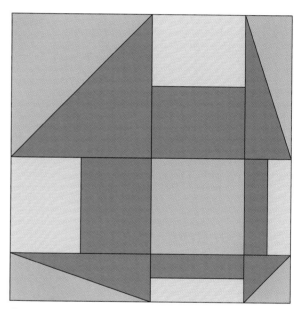

Churn Dash block color combination 2; make 18

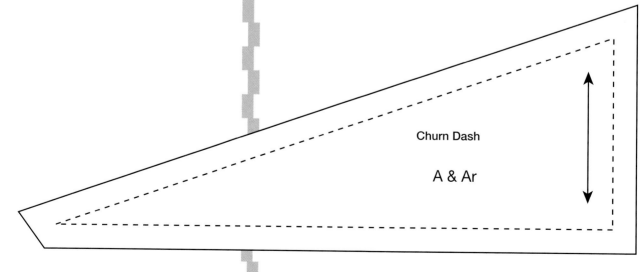

Churn Dash

A & Ar

Quilt assembly

39½" x 39½"

In this quilt, the off-center Arkansas Snowflake blocks are set on-point. Notice how the gold rectangles on two sides of each block create the look of a pseudo-sashing.

Made by Lesley Gray, Bloomington, Illinois.

ARKANSAS SNOWFLAKE

Finished blocks: 6" square

Fabric and Supplies

Off-white	½ yard
Gold	¼ yard
Dark blue	¼ yard
Light green	⅜ yard
Dark green	⅜ yard
Brown	⅛ yard
Blue inner border	⅜ yard
Red outer border	¾ yard
Backing	2 ½ yards
Batting	43" x 43"
Binding	¾ yard

Cutting List

Note: Cut all strips across the 42" fabric width.
Patterns for pieces A, Ar, and B are on page 33.

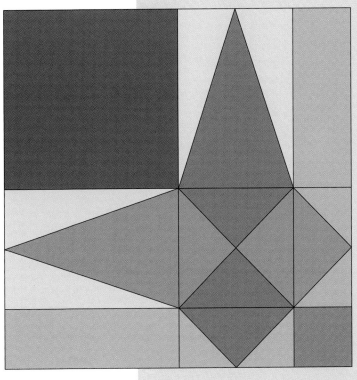

Off-set Arkansas Snowflake block

For Arkansas Snowflake Blocks

Fabric	Quantity	Strip width	Pieces to cut from strips
Off-white	4 strips	1¾"	26 A triangles
			26 Ar triangles
	1 strip	9¾"	Two 9¾" x 9¾" squares
			Two 5⅛" x 5⅛" squares
Gold	1 strip	3½"	26 D rectangles, each 3½" x 1½"
	2 strips	1½"	52 G squares, each 1½" x 1½"
Dark blue	2 strips	3½"	13 C squares, each 3½" x 3½"
Light green	1 strip	4"	13 B triangles
	1 strip	1½"	13 F rectangles, each 1½" x 2½"
	1 strip	3¼"	Seven E squares, each 3¼" x 3¼"
Dark green	1 strip	3⅝"	13 B triangles
	1 strip	1½"	13 F rectangles, each 1½" x 2½"
	1 strip	3¼"	Seven squares, each 3¼" x 3¼"
Brown	1 strip	1½"	13 H squares, each 1½" x 1½"

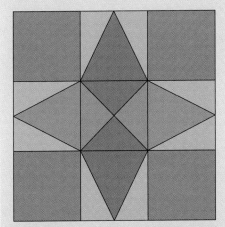

Traditional Arkansas Snowflake block

Cheryl A. Adam OFF CENTER PATCHWORK

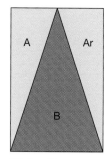

Make 13

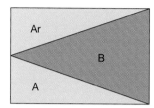

Make 13

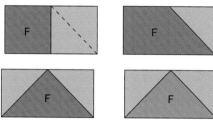

Make 13

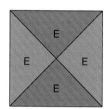

Make 13

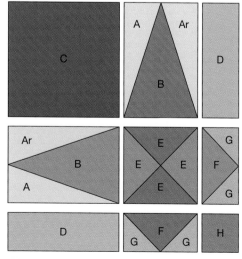

Block assembly

For Borders, Backing, and Binding

Fabric	Quantity	Strip width
Blue		
inner border	4 strips	2½"
Red		
outer border	4 strips	5½"
Backing	2 strips	22" x 43"
Binding	5 strips	desired width

Piecing the Arkansas Snowflake Blocks

1. Sew an off-white A triangle to the left side of a dark green B triangle. Press. Sew an off-white Ar triangle to the right side of the dark green B triangle. Press. Make 13 of these units.

2. Sew an off-white A triangle to the left side of a light green B triangle. Press. Sew an off-white Ar triangle to the right side of the light green B triangle. Press. Make 13 of these units.

3. Draw a diagonal line from corner to corner on the wrong side of the 52 gold G squares. Place a 1½" gold square on one end of a dark green F rectangle, right sides together, and sew on the marked diagonal line. Trim the fabric to a ¼" seam allowance and press the unit open.

4. Place a gold G square at the opposite end of the unit from Step 3, right sides together. Sew on the diagonal marked line. Trim the fabric to a ¼" seam allowance and press the completed unit. Make 13 of the dark green F/G units.

5. Repeat steps 3 and 4 with two gold G squares and a light green F rectangle. Make 13 of the light green F/G units.

6. Cut each of the 3¼" light and dark green squares in quarters diagonally. Sew the light green and dark green E triangles together alternately in pairs. Press. Sew two of these pairs together to form a square. Press. Make 13 of these pieced squares.

7. Referring to the block assembly diagram, sew each block together in three rows. Press. Sew two of these pairs together to form a sqaure. Press. Make 13 Arkansas Snowflake blocks.

Assembling the Quilt Center

1. Cut the two 9¾" x 9¾" off-white squares in quarters diagonally to form the eight side triangles.

2. Cut the two 5⅛" off-white squares in half diagonally to form the four corner triangles.

3. Referring to the quilt assembly diagram, arrange and sew the blocks, side triangles, and corner triangles together in diagonal rows. Press.

4. Sew the diagonal rows together. Press the completed quilt center.

Adding the Borders

1. Referring to the quilt assembly diagram, sew a 2½" wide blue inner border strip to the top and bottom of the quilt center. Press. Trim the excess fabric even with the edges of the quilt center.

2. Sew the remaining two inner border strips to the sides of the quilt center. Press. Trim the excess fabric even with the edges of the quilt center.

3. Sew a 5½"-wide red outer border strip to the top and bottom edges of the quilt center. Press. Trim the excess fabric even with the edges of the quilt center.

4. Sew the remaining two outer border strips to the sides of the quilt center. Press. Trim the excess fabric even with the edges of the quilt.

Finishing

1. Layer the backing, batting, and quilt top. Quilt by hand or machine, as desired.

2. Sew the binding strips together to form one long strip. Fold the binding in half lengthwise, with wrong sides together, and press. Sew the raw edges of the binding to the edges of the front of the quilt. Turn the folded edge of the binding to the back of the quilt and stitch in place by hand, mitering the corner seams.

Quilt assembly

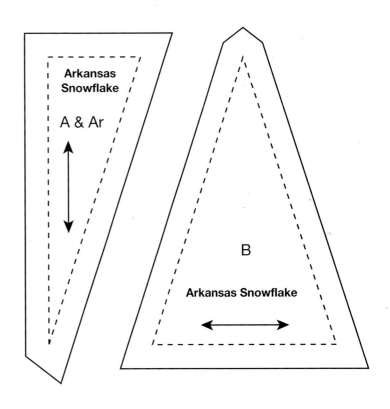

Arkansas Snowflake

A & Ar

B

Arkansas Snowflake

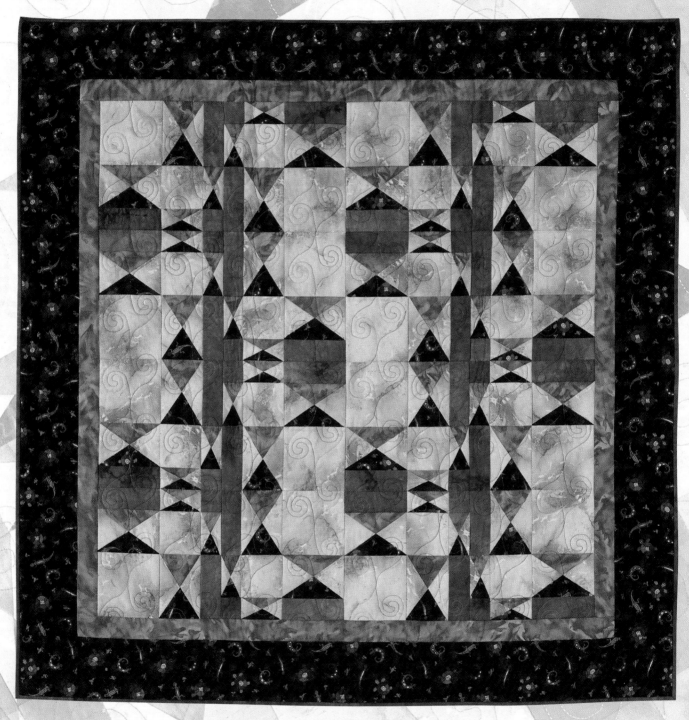

48" x 48"

Four different color combinations of this block are used in this off-center Ohio Star quilt. The blocks are also rotated, which gives the quilt the vertical stripes.

Made by the author.

OHIO STAR

Finished blocks: 9" square

Fabric and Supplies

Cream	1⅜ yards
Rust	½ yard
Navy print	½ yard
Blue	½ yard
Blue inner border	⅜ yard
Navy print outer border	¾ yard
Backing	3 yards
(or 1½ yards of 60"-wide fabric)	
Batting	52" x 52"
Binding	½ yard

Off-set Ohio Star block

Cutting List

Note: Cut all strips across the 42" fabric width. Pattern pieces A, B, C, and D are on pages 38 and 39.

For Ohio Star Blocks

Fabric	Quantity	Strip width	Cut from strips
Cream	2 strips	1½"	32 A triangles
	4 strips	2¼"	32 B triangles
			32 C triangles
	2 strips	2⅞"	32 D triangles
	2 strips	3½"	16 G squares, each 3½" x 3½"
	2 strips	5"	16 H squares, each 5" x 5"
Rust	5 strips	2"	16 E squares, each 2" x 2"
			32 F rectangles, each 2" x 5"
Navy print	1 strip	1½"	16 A triangles
	3 strips	2¼"	16 B triangles
			16 C triangles
	1 strip	2⅞"	16 D triangles
Blue	1 strip	1½"	16 A triangles
	3 strips	2¼"	16 B triangles
			16 C triangles
	1 strip	2⅞"	16 D triangles

For Borders, Backing, and Binding

Blue inner border	4 strips	2"	
Navy print outer border	5 strips	5"	
Backing	2 strips	26" x 52"	
Binding	5 strips	desired width	

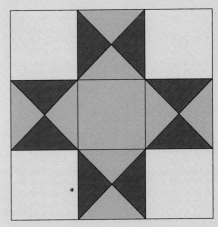

Traditional Ohio Star block

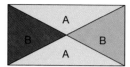

Make 16

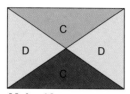

Make 16

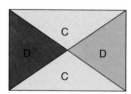

Make 16

Make 16

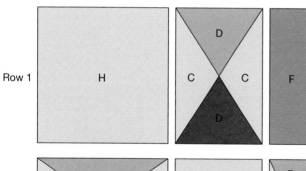

Row 1

Row 2

Row 3

Block assembly

Piecing the Ohio Star Blocks

1. Sew the small rectangles together as shown with the A and B triangles. Press after each seam. Make 16 small rectangles in the two color combinations.

2. Sew the large rectangles together as shown with the C and D triangles. Press after each seam. Make 16 large rectangles in the two color combinations.

3. Referring to the block assembly diagram and the four color combination diagrams on page 37, sew the blocks together in three rows. Press. Sew the rows together, completing the blocks. Press. Make four Ohio Star blocks in each color combination.

Assembling the Quilt Center

1. Sew the Ohio Star blocks together in four rows of four blocks each. Press.

2. Sew the rows together. Press the completed quilt center.

Adding the Borders

1. Referring to the quilt assembly diagram, sew two of the 2"-wide blue inner border strips to the top and bottom of the quilt center. Press. Trim the excess fabric even with the edges of the quilt center.

2. Sew the remaining two inner border strips to the sides of the quilt center. Press. Trim the excess fabric even with the edges of the quilt center.

3. Sew two of the 4¾"-wide navy outer border strips to the top and bottom edges of the quilt center. Press. Trim the excess fabric even with the edges of the quilt center.

4. Cut one of the 4¾"-wide navy strips into two equal pieces. Sew one of the pieces to each of the remaining two full-length outer border strips.

5. Sew the two outer border strips to the sides of the quilt center. Press. Trim excess fabric even with the edges of the quilt.

Finishing

1. Sew the two backing strips together and press the seam allowance open.

2. Layer the backing, batting, and quilt top. Quilt by hand or machine, as desired.

3. Sew the binding strips together to form one long strip. Fold the binding in half lengthwise, with wrong sides together, and press. Sew the raw edges of the binding to the edges of the front of the quilt. Turn the folded edge of the binding to the back of the quilt and stitch in place by hand, mitering the corner seams.

Ohio Star block color combination 1; make 4

Ohio Star block color combination 2; make 4

Ohio Star block color combination 3; make 4

Ohio Star block color combination 4; make 4

Quilt assembly

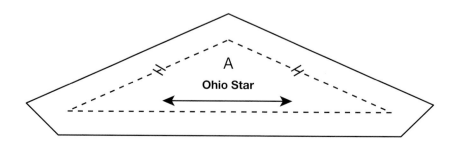

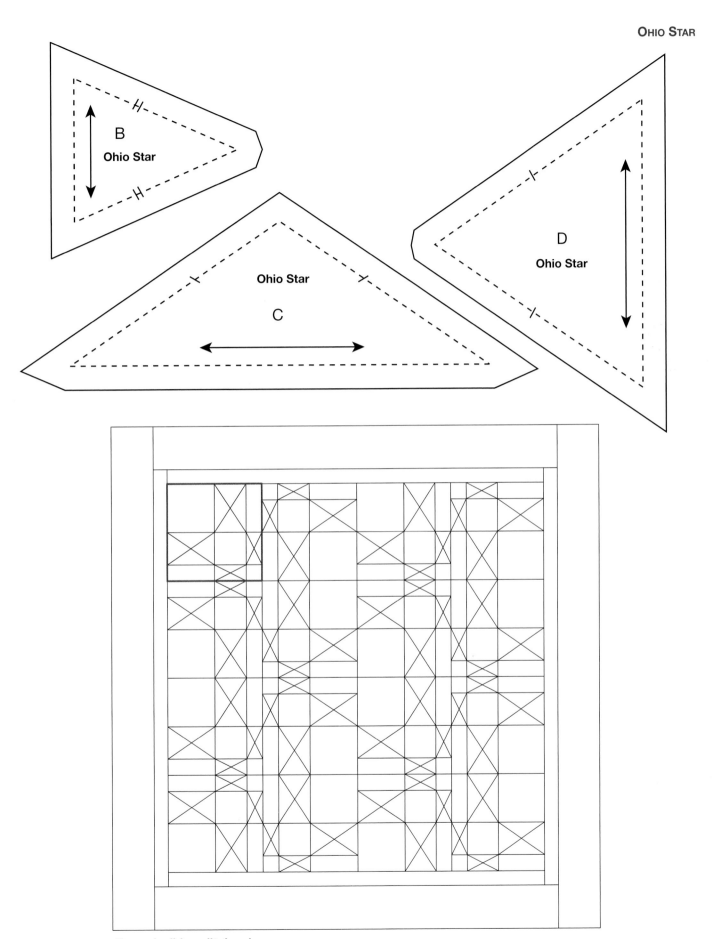

B
Ohio Star

Ohio Star

C

D
Ohio Star

Reproducible quilt drawing

64" x 64"

Half of the off-set Jacob's Ladder blocks in this quilt feature one set of color placements, and the remaining blocks feature another. The two blocks are alternated in the quilt, with one block turned upside down. This gives the appearance of curved lines going diagonally down the quilt.

Made by Evelyn Young, LeRoy, Illinois.

JACOB'S LADDER

Finished blocks: 12" square

Fabric and Supplies

Dark blue	1	yard
Light blue	1	yard
Light green	⅜	yard
Dark green	⅜	yard
Dark red	⅝	yard
Pink	⅝	yard
Pink inner border	½	yard
Dark blue outer border	1 ¼	yards
Backing	4	yards
Batting	68" x 68"	
Binding	¾	yard

Cutting List

Note: Cut all strips across the 42" fabric width.
Patterns for pieces A, Ar, B, and Br are on page 45.

Off-set Jacob's Ladder block

For Jacob's Ladder Blocks

Fabric	Quantity	Strip width	Cut from strips
Dark blue	4 strips	4¾"	16 B triangles
			16 Br triangles
	4 strips	2¾"	16 A triangles
			16 Ar triangles
Light blue	4 strips	4¾"	16 B triangles
			16 Br triangles
	4 strips	2¾"	16 A triangles
			16 Ar triangles
Light green	6 strips	1½"	
Dark green	6 strips	1½"	
Dark red	3 strips	3½"	
	2 strips	2½"	
	2 strips	1½"	
Pink	3 strips	3½"	
	2 strips	2½"	
	2 strips	1½"	

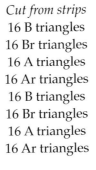

Traditional Jacob's Ladder block

For Borders, Backing, and Binding

Pink inner border	5 strips	2½"
Dark blue outer border	6 strips	6½"
Backing	2 strips	34" x 68"
Binding	7 strips	desired width

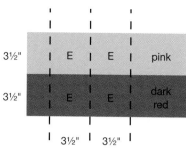

3½"　E　E　pink

3½"　E　E　dark red

3½"　3½"

Cut 32

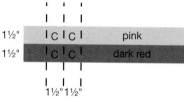

2½"　D　D　pink

2½"　D　D　dark red

2½"　2½"

Cut 32

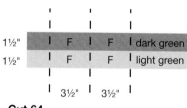

1½"　C　C　pink

1½"　C　C　dark red

1½"　1½"

Cut 32

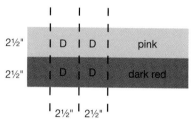

1½"　F　F　dark green

1½"　F　F　light green

3½"　3½"

Cut 64

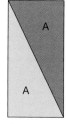

A

A

Make 16

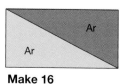

Ar

Ar

Make 16

Piecing the Jacob's Ladder Blocks

1 Sew a 3½"-wide dark red strip to a 3½"-wide pink strip to form a strip-set. Press. Make three of these strip-sets. Cut the strip-sets into 32 – 3½"-wide E segments.

2. Sew a 2½"-wide dark red strip to a 2½"-wide pink strip to form a strip-set. Press. Repeat to make a second strip-set. Cut the strip-sets into 32 – 2½"-wide D segments.

3. Sew a 1½"-wide dark red strip to a 1½"-wide pink strip to form a strip-set. Press. Repeat to make a second strip-set. Cut the strip-sets into 32 – 1½"-wide C segments.

4. Sew a 1½"-wide dark green strip to a 1½"-wide light green strip to form a strip-set. Press. Make six of these strip-sets. Cut the strip-sets into 64 – 3½"-wide F segments.

5. Sew the long edge of a dark blue A triangle to the long edge of a light blue A triangle. Press. Make 16 A/A rectangles.

6. Sew the long edge of a dark blue Ar triangle to the long edge of a light blue Ar triangle. Press. Make 16 Ar/Ar rectangles.

7. Sew the long edge of a dark blue B triangle to the long edge of a light blue B triangle. Press. Make 16 B/B rectangles.

8. Sew the long edge of a dark blue Br triangle to the long edge of a light blue Br triangle. Press. Make 16 Br/Br rectangles.

9. Referring to the block assembly diagram, sew the Jacob's Ladder blocks together in three rows. Press. Sew the rows together to complete each block. Press. Make eight blocks in one color combination and eight blocks in the second color combination (see page 44).

Assembling the Quilt Center

1. Referring to the quilt assembly diagram, sew the Jacob's Ladder blocks together in four rows of four blocks each. Press.

2. Sew the rows of blocks together. Press the completed quilt center.

Adding the Borders

1. Cut one of the 2½"-wide pink inner border strips into four equal pieces. Sew one of the pieces to the end of each of the remaining full-length border strips. Press.

2. Referring to the quilt assembly diagram, sew two inner border strips to the top and bottom of the quilt center. Press. Trim the excess fabric even with the edges of the quilt center.

3. Sew the remaining two inner border strips to the sides of the quilt center. Press. Trim the excess fabric even with the edges of the quilt center.

4. Cut two of the 6½" strips in half. Sew one of the pieces to the end of each of the remaining full-length dark blue outer border strips.

5. Sew two outer border strips to the top and bottom of the quilt center. Press. Trim the excess fabric even with the edges of the quilt center.

6. Sew the remaining two outer border strips to the sides of the quilt center. Press. Trim the excess fabric even with the edges of the quilt.

Finishing

1. Sew the two backing strips together and press the seam allowance open.

2. Layer the backing, batting, and quilt top. Quilt by hand or machine, as desired.

3. Sew the binding strips together to form one long strip. Fold the binding in half lengthwise, with wrong sides together, and press. Sew the raw edges of the binding to the edges of the front of the quilt. Turn the folded edge of the binding to the back of the quilt and stitch in place by hand, mitering the corner seams.

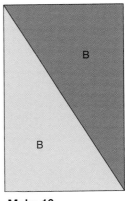

Make 16

Make 16

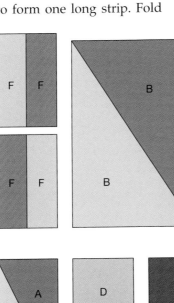

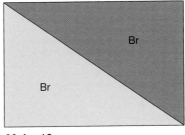

Row 1

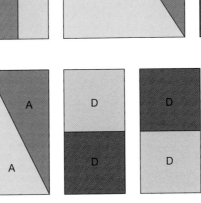

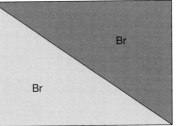

Row 2

  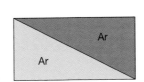 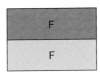 

Block assembly

Row 3

Jacob's Ladder block color combination 1; make 8

Jacob's Ladder block color combination 2; make 8

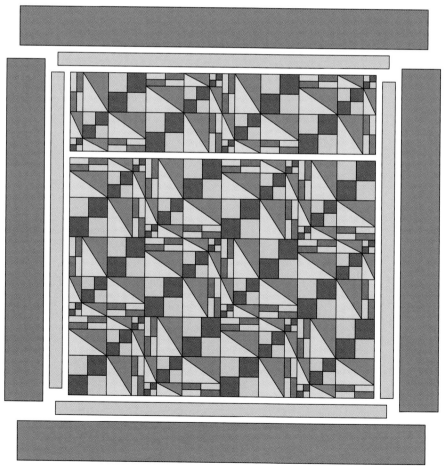

Quilt assembly

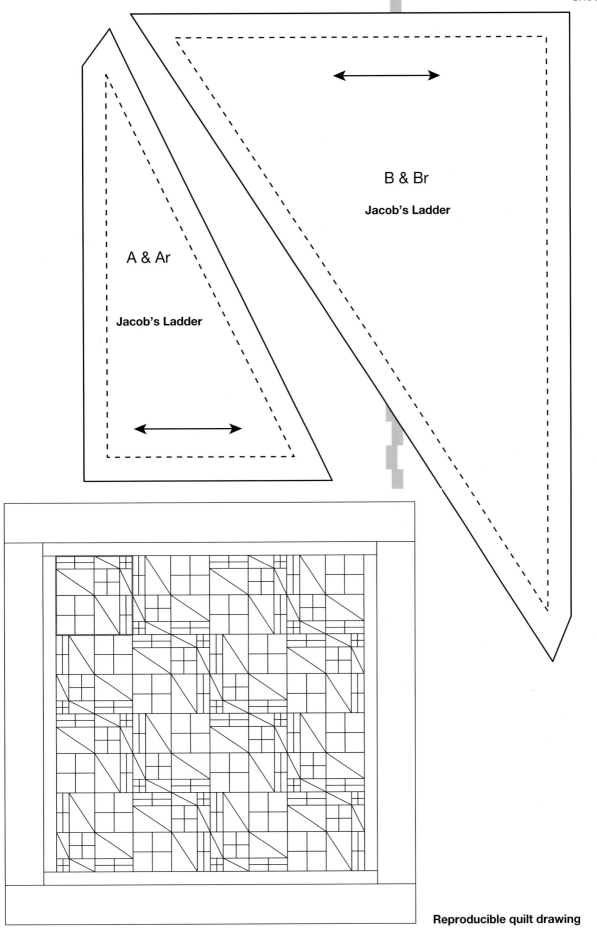

B & Br

Jacob's Ladder

A & Ar

Jacob's Ladder

Reproducible quilt drawing

47" x 47"

The center of the Rosebud block is moved toward a corner, then the block is redrafted. The blocks are all paper pieced. Every other block is rotated by one-quarter turn, and every other row is turned upside down.

Made by Connie Guhlstorf and Anne Powell, both of Normal, Illinois.

ROSEBUD

Finished blocks: 9" square

Fabric and Supplies

Dark green	½ yard
Light green	½ yard
Burgundy	¾ yard
Burgundy print	¾ yard
Peach	1 ¼ yards
Dark green inner border	¼ yard
Light green middle border	¼ yard
Burgundy print outer border	¾ yard
Backing	3 yards
Batting	51" x 51"
Binding	½ yard

Cutting List

Note: Fabric for paper piecing must be cut at least ½" larger than the sections on all sides. Patterns are on pages 49–51.

For Rosebud Blocks

Fabric	Pieces to cut
Dark green	16 Section B-7
	16 Section C-7
Light green	16 each: sections B-2, B-4, and B-6
	16 each: sections C-2, C-4, and C-6
Burgundy	16 each: sections A-2, A-4, and A-6
	16 each: sections D-2, D-4, and D-6
Burgundy print	16 Section A-7
	16 Section D-7
Peach	16 each: sections A-1, A-3, and A-5
	16 each: sections B-1, B-3, and B-5
	16 each: sections C-1, C-3, and C-5
	16 each: sections D-1, D-3, and D-5

For Borders, Backing, and Binding

Fabric	Quantity	Strip width
Dark green inner border	4 strips	1½"
Light green middle border	4 strips	1½"
Burgundy print outer border	5 strips	4"
Backing	2 strips	26" x 51"
Binding	5 strips	desired width

Off-set Rosebud block

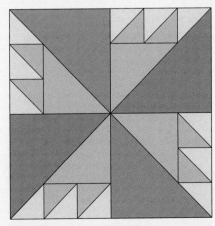

Traditional Rosebud block

Paper-Piecing the Rosebud Blocks

1. Photocopy the paper-piecing patterns from pages 49–51 on lightweight paper. You will need 16 copies of each of the four sections of the Rosebud block.

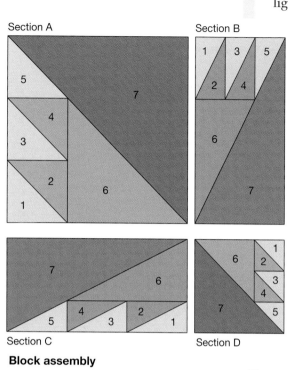

Section A

Section B

2. Cut the fabrics listed for the pieces shown on the pattern sections. Remember to do this from the unmarked side of the paper, and with the right side of the fabrics facing up.

3. For each of the four sections, start by placing fabric #1 on the unmarked side of the pattern, right side up, making sure that it covers the entire area of the pattern piece. Place fabric #2 right side up over its pattern piece, making sure that it covers the entire area of the pattern piece. Carefully flip piece #2 on top of piece #1 so right sides are together, making sure that fabric covers both pieces on the sewing line and creates a ¼" seam allowance. Pin the two fabrics in place. Turn the paper pattern over and stitch on the line between pieces #1 and #2.

4. Flip piece #2 over, so that the right side faces up, press. Check once again to make sure that fabric covers the entire pattern pieces.

Section C

Section D

Block assembly

5. Repeat steps 3 and 4 for the remaining pattern pieces in each of the four sections of the Rosebud block. Use the block assembly diagram as a guide to color placements in each section. When you have completed each section, trim the outside seam allowances to ¼".

6. Sew the paper-pieced sections together to complete each of the 16 Rosebud blocks. Carefully tear off the paper from the back of each block. Press.

Assembling the Quilt Center

1. Referring to the quilt assembly diagram, sew the blocks together in four rows of four blocks each. Press.

2. Sew the rows of blocks together. Press the completed quilt center.

Adding the Borders

1. Referring to the quilt assembly diagram, sew two of the 1½"-wide dark green inner border strips to the top and bottom of the

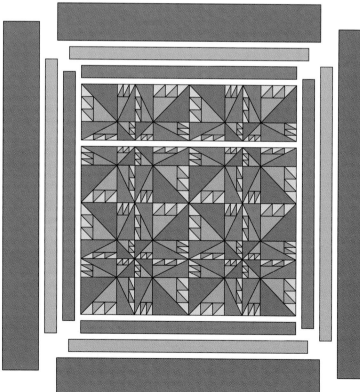

Quilt assembly

quilt center. Press. Trim the excess fabric even with the edges of the quilt center.

2. Sew the remaining two inner border strips to the sides of the quilt center. Press. Trim the excess fabric even with the edges of the quilt center.

3. Sew two of the 1½"-wide light green middle border strips to the top and bottom of the quilt center. Press. Trim the excess fabric even with the edges of the quilt center.

4. Sew the remaining two middle border strips to the sides of the quilt center. Press. Trim the excess fabric even with the edges of the quilt center.

5. Sew two of the 4"-wide burgundy print outer border strips to the top and bottom of the quilt center. Press. Trim the excess fabric even with the edges of the quilt center.

6. Cut one of the outer border strips into two equal pieces. Sew one of the pieces to the end of each of the remaining two full-length outer border strips. Sew the remaining two outer border strips to the sides of the quilt center. Press. Trim the excess fabric even with the edges of the quilt.

Finishing

1. Sew the two backing strips together and press the seam allowance open.

2. Layer the backing, batting, and quilt top. Quilt by hand or machine, as desired.

3. Sew the binding strips together to form one long strip. Fold the binding in half lengthwise, with wrong sides together, and press. Sew the raw edges of the binding to the edges of the front of the quilt. Turn the folded edge of the binding to the back of the quilt and stitch in place by hand, mitering the corner seams.

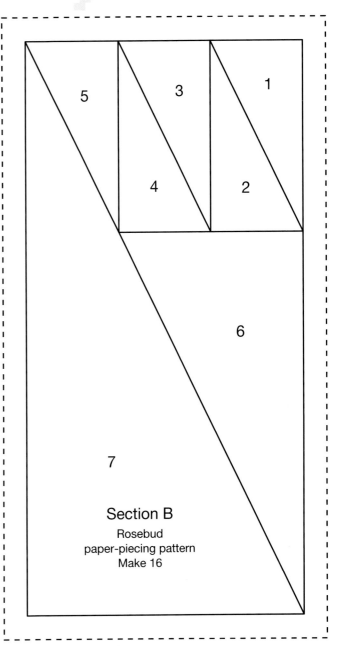

Section B
Rosebud
paper-piecing pattern
Make 16

Solid lines are seam lines

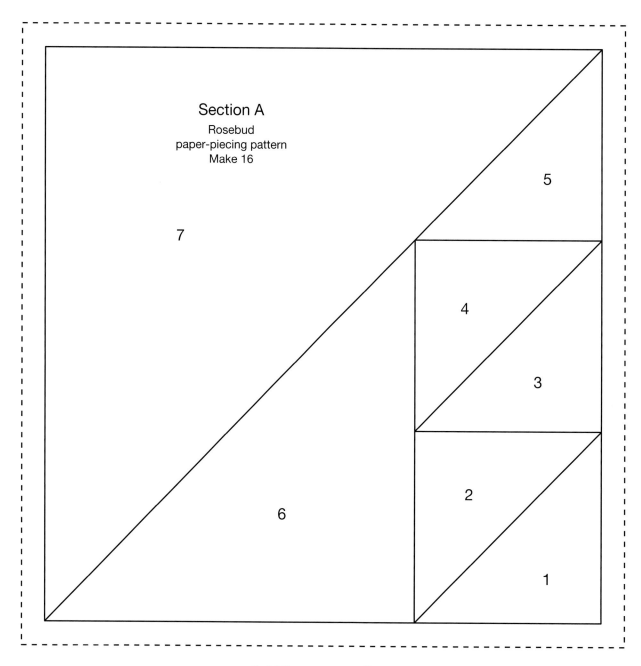

Section A
Rosebud
paper-piecing pattern
Make 16

5

7

4

3

6

2

1

Solid lines are seam lines

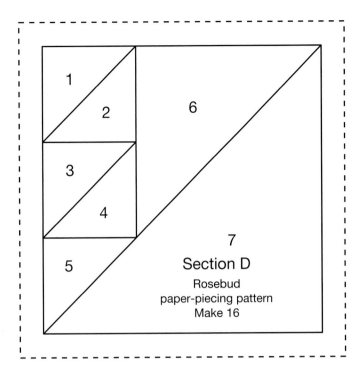

Section D
Rosebud
paper-piecing pattern
Make 16

Solid lines are seam lines

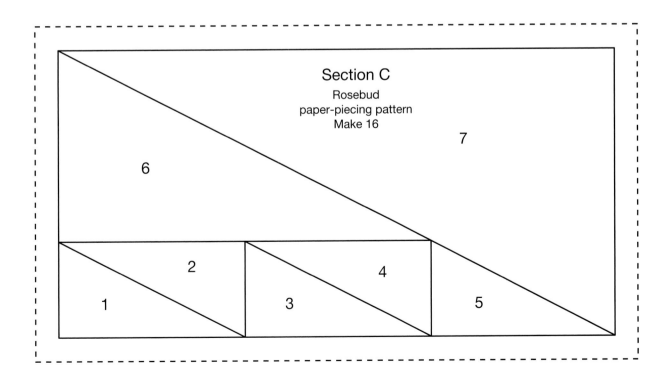

Section C
Rosebud
paper-piecing pattern
Make 16

90" x 90"

This quilt is divided into quarters. All the blocks in each quarter are placed in the same direction, then each of the quarters is rotated to create the final design.

Made by the author.

54-40 OR FIGHT

Finished blocks: 12" square

Fabrics and Supplies

Aqua	¾ yard
Dark blue	3 yards
Dark teal	1 ½ yards
Burgundy	1 ¼ yards
Bright pink	1 ¾ yards
Aqua first and third borders	⅝ yard
Dark teal second border	¾ yard
Dark blue outer border	1 ¾ yards
Backing	8 yards
Batting	94" x 94"
Binding	1 yard

Off-set 54-40 or Fight block

Cutting List

Note: Cut all strips across the 42" fabric width.
Pattern pieces A, Ar, and B are on page 57.

For 54-40 or Fight Blocks

Fabric	Quantity	Strip width	Cut from strips
Aqua	5 strips	4½"	72 G rectangles, each 4½" x 2½"
Dark blue	9 strips	2½"	144 H squares, each 2½" x 2½"
	12 strips	1½"	
	20 strips	2⅝"	72 A triangles
			72 Ar triangles
Dark teal	8 strips	6⅝"	72 B triangles
Burgundy	6 strips	3½"	
	5 strips	2½"	
	3 strips	1½"	
Bright pink	6 strips	3½"	
	5 strips	2½"	
	3 strips	1½"	
	12 strips	1½"	

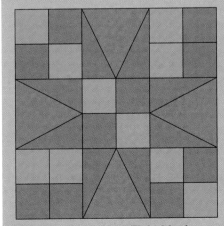

Traditional 54-40 or Fight block

For Borders, Backing, and Binding

Aqua first and third borders	16 strips	1"
Dark teal second border	8 strips	2½"
Dark blue outer border	9 strips	6½"
Backing	3 strips	32" x 94"
Binding	10 strips	desired width

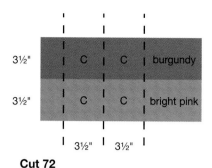

3½" burgundy
3½" bright pink
3½" 3½"

Cut 72

2½" burgundy
2½" bright pink
2½" 2½"

Cut 72

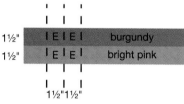

1½" burgundy
1½" bright pink
1½" 1½"

Cut 72

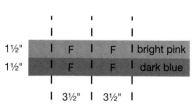

1½" bright pink
1½" dark blue
3½" 3½"

Cut 144

Make 72

Make 72

Piecing the 54-40 or Fight Blocks

1. Sew a 3½"-wide burgundy strip to a 3½"-wide bright pink strip to form a strip-set. Press. Make six of these strip-sets and cut them into 72 C segments, each 3½" wide.

2. Sew a 2½"-wide burgundy strip to a 2½"-wide bright pink strip to form a strip-set. Press. Make five of these strip-sets and cut them into 72 D segments, each 2½" wide.

3. Sew a 1½"-wide burgundy strip to a 1½"-wide bright pink strip to form a strip-set. Make three of these strip-sets and cut them into 72 E segments, each 1½" wide.

4. Sew a 1½"-wide bright pink strip to a 1½"-wide dark blue strip to form a strip-set. Press. Make 12 of these strip-sets and cut them into 144 F segments, each 3½" wide as shown. Note: If desired, you can cut these strip sets into 72 F segments, each 6½" wide, to eliminate the seam between these segments in the finished blocks.

5. Draw a diagonal line, from corner to corner on the back of the 144 dark blue 2½" H squares. Place a dark blue square at one end of a 2½" x 4½" aqua G rectangle with right sides together. Sew on the marked diagonal line. Trim away the excess fabric, leaving a ¼" seam allowance. Open the unit and press.

6. Place another 2½" dark blue square at the opposite end of the same 2½" x 4½" aqua rectangle and sew them together as in Step 5. Open the unit and press. Make 72 of these units.

7. Sew a dark blue A triangle to the left side of a dark teal B triangle. Press. Sew a dark blue Ar triangle to the right side of the dark teal B triangle. Press. Make 72 of these pieced rectangles.

8. Referring to the block assembly diagram, sew each block together in three rows. Press. Sew the rows together to complete each block. Make thirty-six 54-40 or Fight blocks.

Assembling the Quilt Center

1. Referring to the quilt assembly diagram, sew the blocks together in six rows of six blocks each. Press.

2. Sew the rows of blocks together. Press the completed quilt center.

Adding the Borders

1. Sew the sixteen 1"-wide aqua strips together in pairs to make 8 strips for the first and third borders.

2. Referring to the quilt assembly diagram, sew two of the first border strips to the top and bottom of the quilt center. Press. Trim the excess fabric even with the edges of the quilt center.

3. Sew two more first border strips to the sides of the quilt center. Press. Trim the excess fabric even with the edges of the quilt center.

4. Sew the eight 2½"-wide dark teal strips together in pairs to make four strips for the second border.

5. Sew two of the second border strips to the top and bottom of the quilt center. Press. Trim the excess fabric even with the edges of the quilt center.

6. Sew the remaining two second border strips to the sides of the quilt center. Press. Trim the excess fabric even with the edges of the quilt center.

7. Sew two of the 1"-wide aqua third border strips to the top and bottom of the quilt center. Press. Trim the excess fabric even with the edges of the quilt center.

8. Sew the remaining two third border strips to the sides of the quilt center. Press. Trim the excess fabric even with the edges of the quilt center.

9. Sew eight of the 6½"-wide dark blue strips together in pairs to make four strips for the outer borders. Cut the remaining 6½" strip in half and add the pieces to two of the joined strips.

10. Sew the shorter two outer border strips to the top and bottom of the quilt center. Press. Trim the excess fabric even with the edges of the quilt center.

11. Sew the longer two outer border strips to the sides of the quilt center. Press. Trim the excess fabric even with the edges of the quilt center.

Finishing

1. Sew the three backing strips together and press the seam allowances open.

2. Layer the backing, batting, and quilt top. Quilt by hand or machine, as desired.

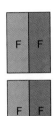

Make 72

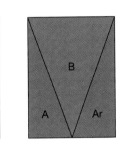

Row 1

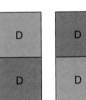

Row 2

Row 3

Block assembly

3. Sew the binding strips together to form one long strip. Fold the binding in half lengthwise, with wrong sides together, and press. Sew the raw edges of the binding to the edges of the front of the quilt. Turn the folded edge of the binding to the back of the quilt and stitch in place by hand, mitering the corner seams.

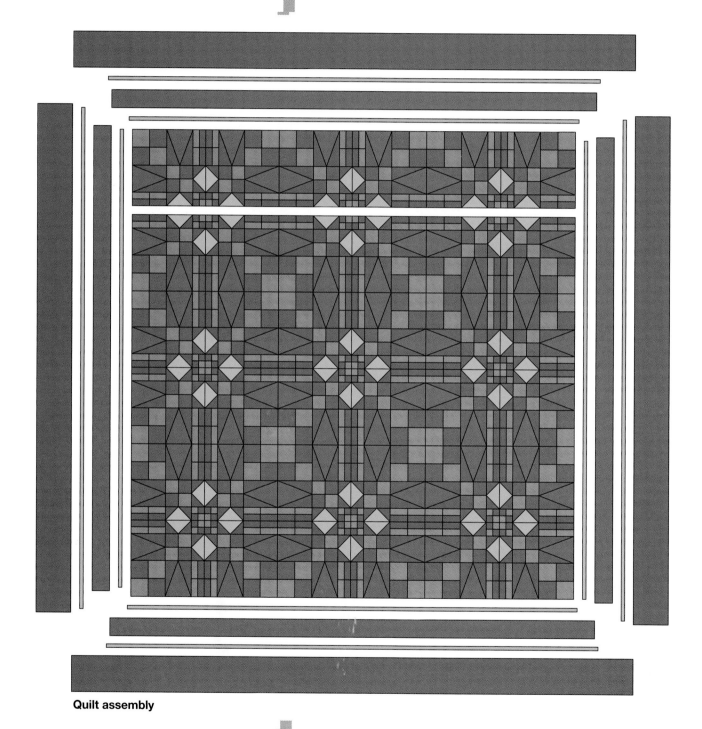

Quilt assembly

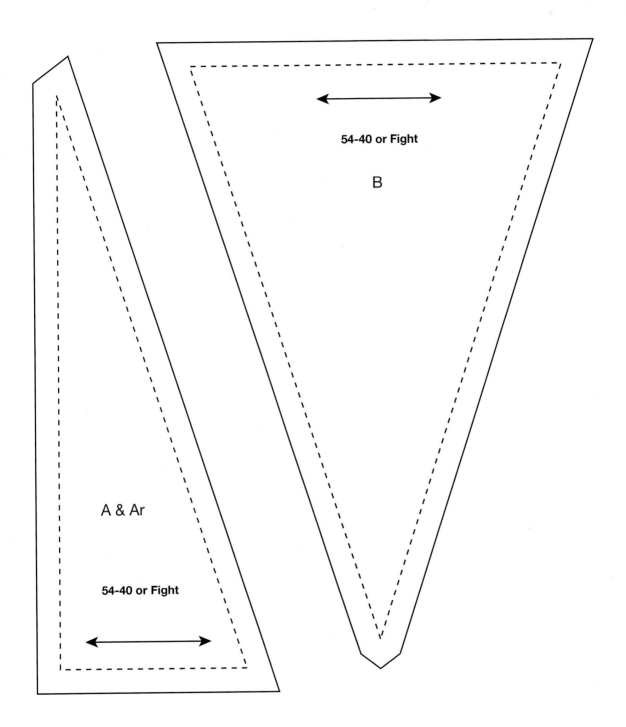

54-40 or Fight

B

A & Ar

54-40 or Fight

62" x 62"

Four Sawtooth blocks in this quilt are rotated a quarter-turn to form a single, large star-like block. Notice how two of the triangles at the center of the quilt feature different fabrics for added visual interest.   Made by the author.

SAWTOOTH

Finished blocks: 12" square

Fabrics and Supplies

Blue	1 ¼ yards
Brown	1 ¼ yards
Brown print	⅞ yard
Tan	1 ⅜ yards
Blue inner border	⅜ yard
Brown print outer border	1 yard
Backing	3 ⅞ yards
Batting	66" x 66"
Binding	⅝ yard

Cutting List

Note: Cut all strips across the 42" fabric width. Fabric for paper piecing must be cut at least ½" larger than the sections on all sides. Pattern pieces C and Cr are on page 63. Paper-piecing patterns are on pages 63 and 64.

Off-set Sawtooth block

For Sawtooth Blocks

Fabric	Quantity	Strip width	Cut from strips
Brown	3 strips	2¾"	16 C triangles
			16 Cr triangles
	3 strips	2½"	32 each: sections E-2, E-3, E-4, and E-5
	1 strip	2⅞"	8 F squares, 2⅞" x 2⅞"
	2 strips	6⅞"	1 A square, 6⅞" x 6⅞"
			16 of Section D-5
Blue	4 strips	6½"	32 of Section B-1
	2 strips	4½"	32 of Section E-1
Brown print	2 strips	6⅞"	8 A squares, 6⅞" x 6⅞"
	1 strip	2⅞"	8 F squares, 2⅞" x 2⅞"
	2 strips	3½"	16 of Section D-1
Tan	2 strips	6⅞"	7 A squares, 6⅞" x 6⅞"
	3 strips	2¾"	16 C triangles
			16 Cr triangles
	4 strips	3½"	32 each: sections B-2, B-3, B-4, and B-5
	2 strips	2½"	16 each: sections D-2, D-3, and D-4

Traditional Sawtooth block

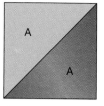

Make 14   **Make 2**

Make 16

Make 16

Make 16

For Borders, Backing, and Binding

Fabric	Quantity	Strip width
Blue inner border	5 strips	2½"
Brown print outer border	6 strips	5½"
Backing	2 strips	33" x 66"
Binding	7 strips	desired width

Piecing the Sawtooth Blocks

1. Mark a diagonal line on the wrong side of the 6⅞" brown print A squares. Place a marked brown print A square and a 6⅞" tan (or brown) A square right sides together and sew a ¼" seam on each side of the marked line. Cut through both fabrics on the diagonal line to make two half-square triangles. Press. Make 14 brown print/tan half-square triangles and two brown print/brown half-square triangles. The pieced squares should measure 6½" x 6½".

2. Repeat Step 1 with the 2⅞" brown print squares and 2⅞" brown squares. Press. Make 16 brown print/brown half-square triangles. The pieced squares should measure 2½" x 2½".

3. With right sides together, sew the long edge of a tan C triangle to the long edge of a brown C triangle. Press. Make 16 C/C rectangles.

4. With right sides together, sew the long edge of a tan Cr triangle to the long edge of a brown Cr triangle. Press. Make 16 Cr/Cr rectangles.

5. Copy the paper-piecing patterns onto lightweight paper. You will need 32 photocopies of sections B and E, and 16 copies of Section D.

6. Cut the fabrics listed for the paper-pieced sections. Remember to do this from the unmarked side of the paper and with the right side of the fabrics facing up.

7. For each section, place piece #1 on the unmarked side of the paper pattern, right side up, making sure it covers the entire area of the pattern piece. Place piece #2, right side up, positioning it so it covers its pattern piece. Carefully flip piece #2 over onto piece #1, so that the right sides are together, making sure that fabric from both pieces is positioned on the sewing lines to allow for the seam allowances. Pin the pieces in place on the pattern. Turn the pattern over and stitch on the line between pieces #1 and #2.

Section B

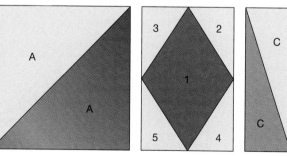

Row 1

Section B

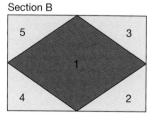

Section D

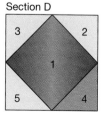

Row 2

Section E

Section E

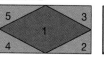

Row 3

Block assembly

8. Flip piece #2 over, so that the right side is facing up, and press. Check again to make sure that the fabric of piece #2 covers the entire pattern piece.

9. Repeat steps 7 and 8 for the remaining pattern pieces in sections B, E, and D.

10. When you have completed piecing each section, trim the outside seam allowances to ¼".

11. Referring to the block assembly diagram, assemble each Sawtooth block in rows, using the paper-pieced sections and the remaining pieces. Press. Sew the rows together to complete the Sawtooth block. Press. Make 16 Sawtooth blocks. Note: Two of these blocks should have 6½" brown print/brown squares and 14 blocks should have 6½" brown print/tan squares. All other colors are the same in every block. Carefully remove the paper from the back of each block, being careful not to stretch the fabric.

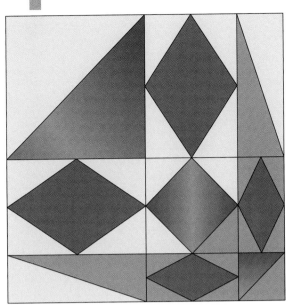

Sawtooth block with 6½" brown print/tan squares; make 14

Assembling the Quilt Center

1. Referring to the quilt assembly diagram, sew the blocks together in four rows of four blocks each. Press.

2. Sew the rows of blocks together. Press the completed quilt center.

Adding the Borders

1. Cut one of the 2½"-wide blue inner border strips into four equal pieces. Sew one of the pieces to the end of each of the remaining full-length border strips. Press.

2. Referring to the quilt assembly diagram, sew two of the inner border strips to the top and bottom of the quilt center. Press. Trim the excess fabric even with the edges of the quilt center.

Sawtooth block with 6½" brown print/brown squares; make 2

3. Sew the remaining two inner border strips to the sides of the quilt center. Press. Trim the excess fabric even with the edges of the quilt center.

4. Cut two of the 5½"-wide brown print outer border strips into two equal pieces. Sew one of the pieces to the end of each of the remaining four full-length outer border strips. Press.

5. Sew two of the outer border strips to the top and bottom of the quilt center. Press. Trim the excess fabric even with the edges of the quilt center.

6. Sew the remaining two outer border strips to the sides of the quilt center. Press. Trim the excess fabric even with the edges of the quilt.

Finishing

1. Sew the two backing strips together and press the seam allowances open.

2. Layer the backing, batting, and quilt top. Quilt by hand or machine, as desired.

3. Sew the binding strips together to form one long strip. Fold the binding in half lengthwise, with wrong sides together, and press. Sew the raw edges of the binding to the edges of the front of the quilt. Turn the folded edge of the binding to the back of the quilt and stitch in place by hand, mitering the corner seams.

Quilt assembly

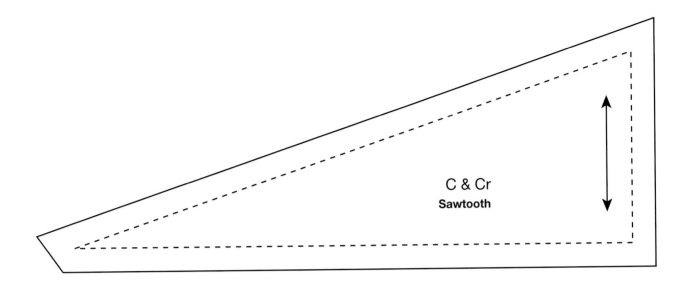

C & Cr
Sawtooth

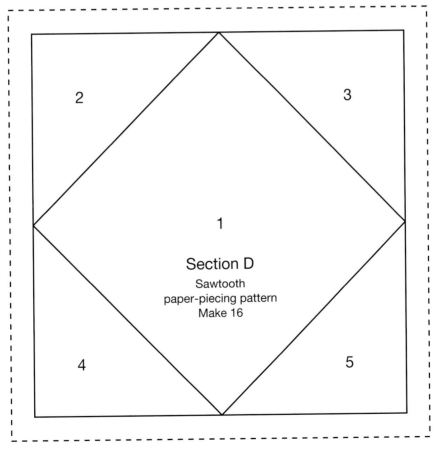

2

3

1

Section D

Sawtooth
paper-piecing pattern
Make 16

4

5

Solid lines are seam lines

Cheryl A. Adam **OFF CENTER PATCHWORK**

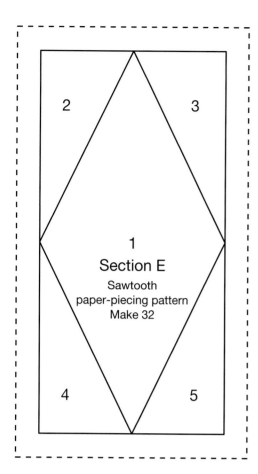

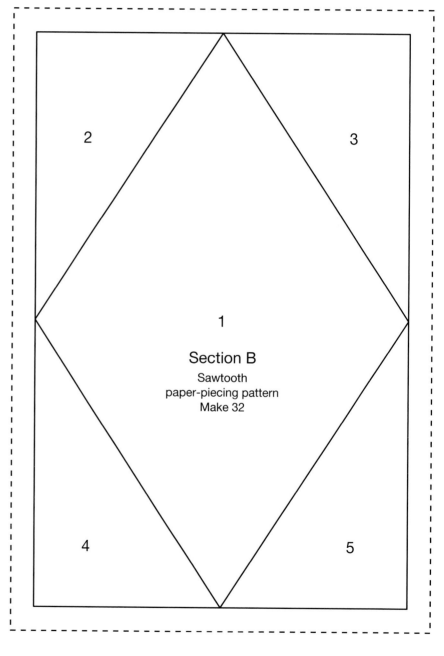

Solid lines are seam lines

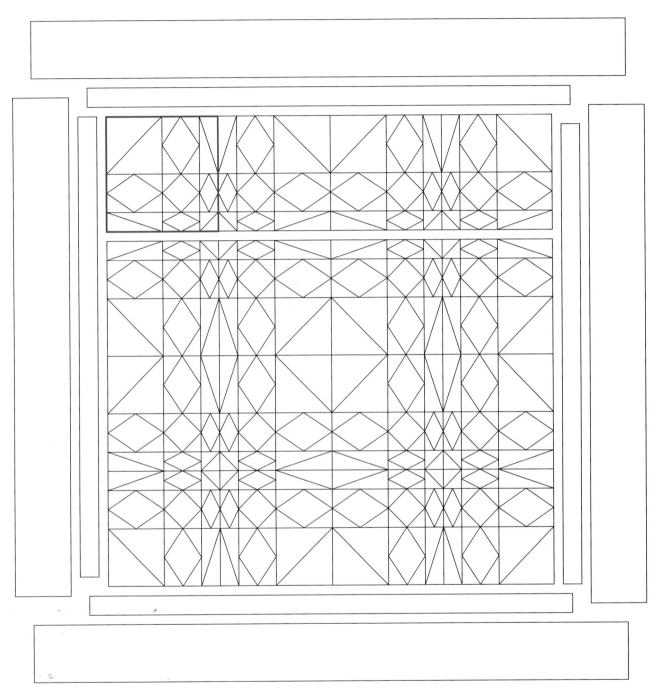

Reproducible quilt drawing

44" x 44"

The blocks in this quilt are paper-pieced, using two different color placement charts. The blocks are alternated and rotated by a quarter-turn to create the quilt design.

Made by Connie Guhlstorf, Normal, Illinois.

CAT'S CRADLE

Finished blocks: 16" square

Fabrics and Supplies

Red	⅝ yard
Gold	⅜ yard
Red print	¼ yard
Gold print	⅝ yard
Blue-gray	⅞ yard
Red print inner border	¼ yard
Gold print outer border	⅞ yard
Backing	3 yards
Batting	48" x 48"
Binding	½ yard

Cutting List

Fabric for paper piecing must be cut at least ½" larger than the sections on all sides. Paper-piecing patterns are on pages 70–73.

For Cat's Cradle Blocks

Fabric	Quantity and pieces to cut
Red	4 each: sections A-2, A-3, and A-4
	4 each: sections Ar-2, Ar-3, and Ar-4
	4 of Section B-5
	4 of Section Br-5
	2 F squares, each 3⅛" x 3⅛"
Gold	4 of Section A-1
	4 of Section Ar-1
	4 each: sections B-2, B-3, and B-4
	4 each: sections Br-2, Br-3, and Br-4
Red print	4 of Section B-1
	4 of Section Br-1
	4 of Section C-1
	4 of Section Cr-1
Gold print	4 each: sections C-2, C-3, and C-4
	4 each: sections Cr-2, Cr-3, and Cr-4
	2 F squares, each 3⅛" x 3⅛"
	4 E squares, each 5⅞" x 5⅞"
Blue-gray	4 of Section A-5
	4 of Section Ar-5
	4 of Section C-5
	4 of Section Cr-5
	4 D squares, each 8½" x 8½"

Off-set Cat's Cradle block

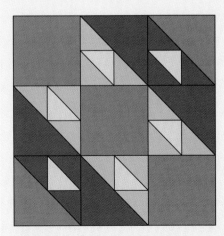

Traditional Cat's Cradle block

For Borders, Backing, and Binding

Note: Cut all strips across the 42" fabric width.

Fabric	Quantity	Strip width
Red print inner border	4 strips	1½"
Gold print outer border	5 strips	5½"
Backing	2 strips	24" x 48"
Binding	5 strips	desired width

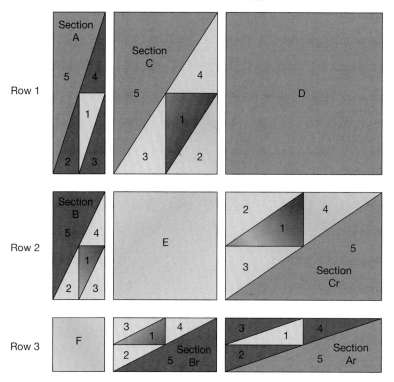

Block assembly

Paper-Piecing the Cat's Cradle Blocks

1. Photocopy the paper-piecing patterns on pages 70–73 onto lightweight paper. You will need four photocopies of each of the six sections for this quilt.

2. Cut the fabrics and pieces listed for the six pattern sections. Remember to do this from the unmarked side of the paper, with the right side of the fabrics facing up.

3. For each paper-pieced section, place piece #1 on the unmarked side of the paper pattern, right side up, making sure that it covers the entire area of the pattern piece. Place piece #2, right side up, positioning it so that it covers its pattern piece. Carefully flip piece #2 over onto piece #1, so that the right sides are together, making sure that fabric from both pieces covers the sewing line and allows for the seam allowances. Pin the pieces in place. Turn the paper pattern over and sew on the line between pieces #1 and #2.

4. Flip piece #2 over, so that the right side is facing up, and press. Check again to make sure that fabric covers the entire pattern piece.

5. Repeat steps 3 and 4 for the remaining pattern pieces in each of the six sections. When you have completed piecing each section, trim the outside seam allowances to ¼".

6. Referring to the block assembly diagram, assemble each Cat's Cradle block in rows, using the paper-pieced sections and fabric squares. Press. Sew the rows together to complete the block. Press. Make four Cat's Cradle blocks. Note: Two of the blocks will have red print 3⅛" squares and two will have gold print 3⅛" squares. All other coloring is the same in all four blocks. Carefully remove the paper from the back of each block, being careful not to stretch the fabric.

Assembling the Quilt Center

1. Referring to the quilt assembly diagram, sew the blocks together in two rows of two blocks each. Press.

2. Sew the rows of blocks together. Press the completed quilt center.

Adding the Borders

1. Sew two of the 1½"-wide red print inner border strips to the top and bottom of the quilt center. Press. Trim the excess fabric even with the edges of the quilt center.

2. Sew the remaining two inner border strips to the sides of the quilt center. Press. Trim the excess fabric even with the edges of the quilt center.

3. Sew two of the 5½"-wide gold print outer border strips to the top and bottom of the quilt center. Press. Trim the excess fabric even with the edges of the quilt center.

4. Cut one of the 5½"-wide outer border strips into two equal pieces. Sew one of the pieces to the end of each of the remaining two full-length outer border strips.

5. Sew the remaining two outer border strips to the sides of the quilt. Press. Trim the excess fabric even with the edges of the quilt center.

Finishing

1. Sew the two backing strips together and press the seam allowances open.

2. Layer the backing, batting, and quilt top. Quilt by hand or machine, as desired.

3. Sew the binding strips together to form one long strip. Fold the binding in half lengthwise, with wrong sides together, and press. Sew the raw edges of the binding to the edges of the front of the quilt. Turn the folded edge of the binding to the back of the quilt and stitch in place by hand, mitering the corner seams.

Quilt assembly

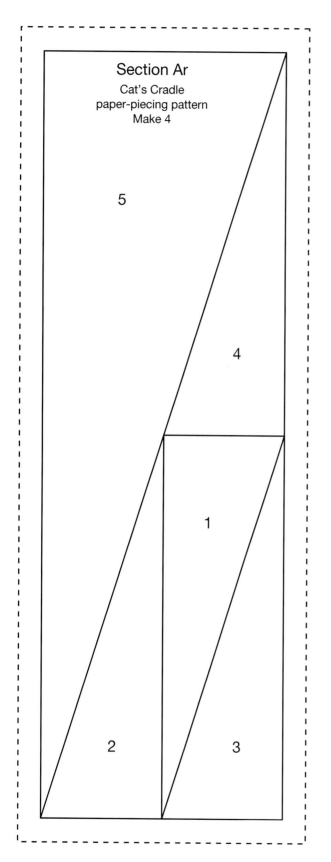

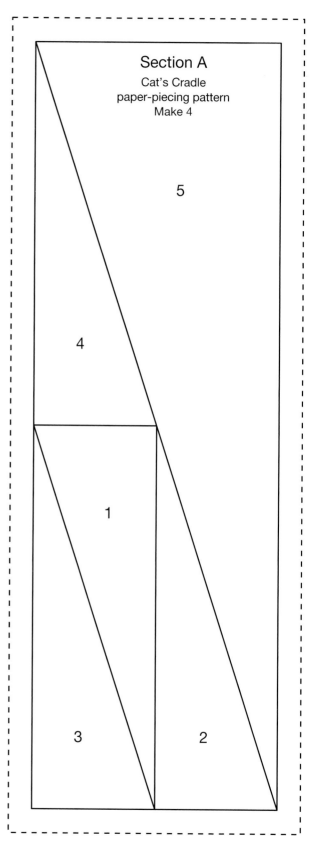

Solid lines are seam lines

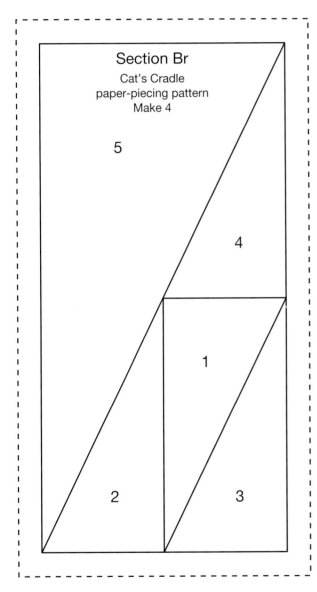

Section Br
Cat's Cradle
paper-piecing pattern
Make 4

5

4

1

2   3

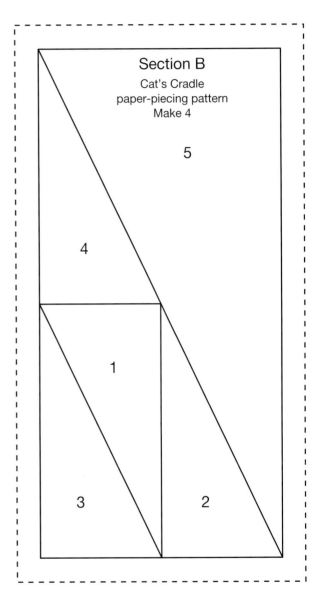

Section B
Cat's Cradle
paper-piecing pattern
Make 4

5

4

1

3   2

Solid lines are seam lines

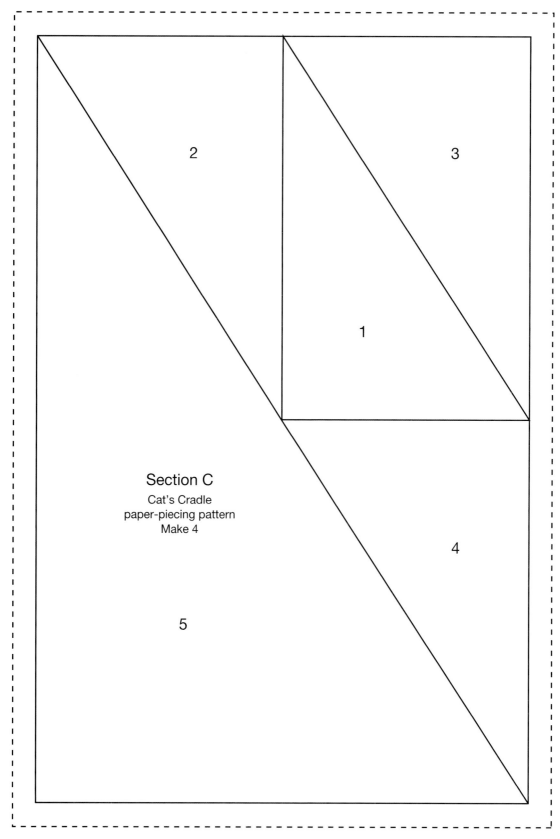

Section C
Cat's Cradle
paper-piecing pattern
Make 4

2

3

1

4

5

Solid lines are seam lines

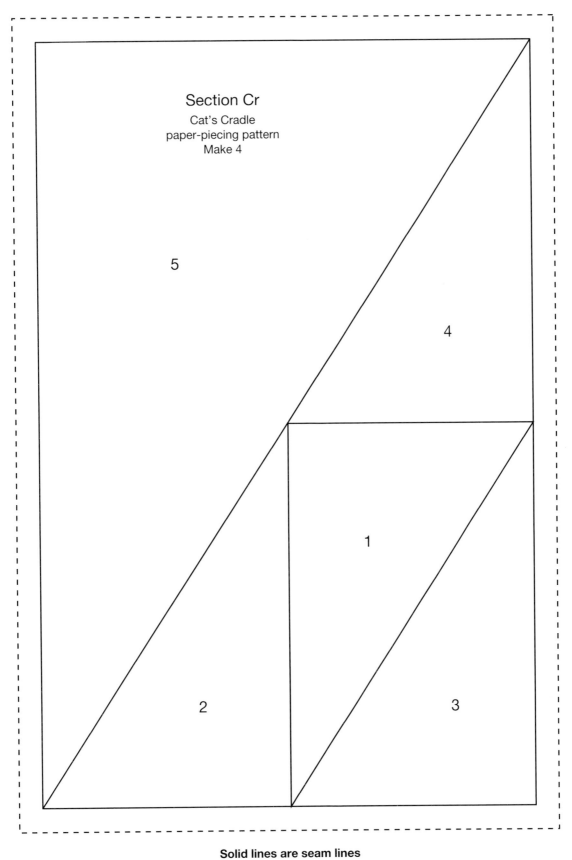

Section Cr
Cat's Cradle
paper-piecing pattern
Make 4

Solid lines are seam lines

64" x 64"

Rotating four blocks by a quarter-turn and sewing them together makes a larger block, which is beautiful in itself. Sewing four of these larger blocks together creates a gorgeous, contemporary quilt design with traditional roots.

Made by Marjorie Blunier, Roanoke, Illinois.

LADY OF THE LAKE

Finished blocks: 12" square

Fabrics and Supplies

Blue	2 yards
Floral	¾ yard
Dark purple	¼ yard
Medium yellow	⅜ yard
Light yellow	⅜ yard
Medium purple	⅜ yard
Light purple	⅜ yard
Dark purple inner border	⅜ yard
Blue outer border	1 ½ yards
Backing	4 yards
Batting	68" x 68"
Binding	¾ yard

Cutting List

Note: Cut all strips across the 42" fabric width.
Pattern pieces A, Ar, B, Br, C, and Cr are on pages 78–79.

For Lady of the Lake Blocks

Fabric	Quantity	Strip width	Pieces to cut
Blue	2 strips	8⅞"	8 E squares, each 8⅞"x 8⅞"
	1 strip	1⅞"	8 F squares, each 1⅞"x 1⅞"
	1 strip	3⅞"	8 D squares, each 3⅞"x 3⅞"
	8 strips	3"	64 A triangles 64 Ar triangles
	9 strips	1¾"	64 B triangles 64 Br triangles 16 C triangles 16 Cr triangles
Floral	2 strips	8⅞"	8 E squares, each 8⅞"x 8⅞"
	1 strip	1⅞"	8 F squares, each 1⅞"x 1⅞"
	1 strip	3⅞"	8 D squares, each 3⅞"x 3⅞"
Dark purple	2 strips	1¾"	16 C triangles 16 Cr triangles

Off-set Lady of the Lake block

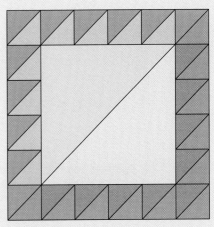

Traditional Lady of the Lake block

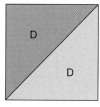

Make 16

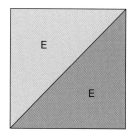

Make 16

Make 16

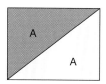

Make 16

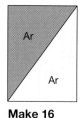

Make 16

Fabric	Quantity	Strip width	Pieces to cut
Medium yellow	2 strips	3"	
	2 strips	1¾"	16 A triangles 16 Ar triangles 16 B triangles 16 Br triangles
Light yellow	2 strips	3"	16 A triangles 16 Ar triangles
	2 strips	1¾"	16 B triangles 16 Br triangles
Medium purple	2 strips	3"	16 A triangles 16 Ar triangles
	2 strips	1¾"	16 B triangles 16 Br triangles
Light purple	2 strips	3"	16 A triangles 16 Ar triangles
	2 strips	1¾"	16 B triangles 16 Br triangles

For Borders, Backing, and Binding

Dark purple inner border	5 strips	2½" wide	
Blue outer border	7 strips	6½"	
Backing	2 strips	34" x 68"	
Binding	7 strips	desired width	

Piecing the Lady of the Lake Blocks

1. Mark a diagonal on the wrong side of the D floral squares. Place a floral and a blue D square right sides together. Sew a ¼" seam on each side of the marked diagonal line. Cut along the diagonal line to make two half-square triangles. Press. Make 16 floral/blue half-square triangles. The pieced squares should measure 3½" x 3½".

2. Repeat Step 1 with the E floral and blue squares. Make 16 floral/blue half-square triangles. The pieced squares should measure 8½" x 8½".

3. Repeat Step 1 with the floral and blue F squares. Make 16 floral/blue half-square triangles. The pieced squares should measure 1½" x 1½".

4. With right sides together, sew the long edge of a blue A triangle to the long edge of a medium yellow A triangle. Press. Make 16 blue/medium yellow A/A rectangles.

5. With right sides together, sew the long edge of a blue Ar tri-

angle to the long edge of a medium yellow Ar triangle. Press. Make 16 blue/medium yellow Ar/Ar rectangles.

6. Repeat Step 4 with each of 16 pairs of blue/light yellow, blue/medium purple, and blue/light purple A triangles.

7. Repeat Step 5 with each of 16 pairs of blue/light yellow, blue/medium purple, and blue/light purple Ar triangles.

8. With right sides together, sew the long edge of a blue B triangle to the long edge of a medium yellow B triangle. Press. Make 16 blue/medium yellow B/B rectangles.

9. With right sides together, sew the long edge of a blue Br triangle to the long edge of a medium yellow Br triangle. Press. Make 16 blue/medium yellow Br/Br rectangles.

10. Repeat Step 8 with each of 16 pairs of blue/light yellow, blue/medium purple, and blue/light purple B triangles. Press.

11. Repeat Step 9 with each of 16 pairs of blue/light yellow, blue/medium purple, and blue/light purple Br triangles. Press.

12. With right sides together, sew the long edge of a blue C triangle to the long edge of a dark purple C triangle. Press. Make 16 blue/dark purple C/C rectangles.

13. With right sides together, sew the long edge of a blue Cr triangle to the long edge of a dark purple Cr triangle. Press. Make 16 blue/dark purple Cr/Cr rectangles.

14. Referring to the block assembly diagram, sew the Lady of the Lake blocks together. Press. Make 16 blocks.

Assembling the Quilt Center

1. Referring to the quilt assembly diagram, sew the blocks together in four rows of four blocks each. Press.

2. Sew the rows of blocks together. Press the completed quilt center.

Adding the Borders

1. Cut one of the 2½"-wide dark purple inner border strips into four equal pieces. Sew one of the pieces to the end of each of the remaining full-length border strips.

2. Sew two of the inner border strips to the top and bottom of the quilt center. Press. Trim the excess fabric even with the edges of the quilt center.

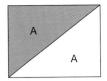

Make 16

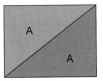

Make 16

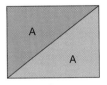

Make 16

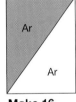

Make 16   Make 16

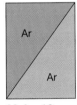

Make 16

Make 16

Make 16

Make 16   Make 16

Make 16

Make 16

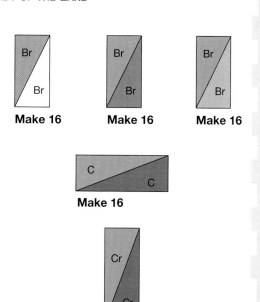

Make 16   **Make 16**   **Make 16**

Make 16

Make 16

3. Sew the remaining two inner border strips to the sides of the quilt center. Press. Trim the excess fabric even with the edges of the quilt center.

4. Cut one of the 6½"-wide blue outer border strips into two equal pieces. Sew one of the pieces to the end of two full-length outer border strips.

5. Sew the two outer border strips from Step 4 to the top and bottom of the quilt center. Press. Trim the excess fabric even with the edges of the quilt center.

6. Sew the remaining four outer border strips in pairs to make two long strips.

7. Sew the two outer border strips from Step 6 to the sides of the quilt center. Press. Trim the excess fabric even with the edges of the quilt center.

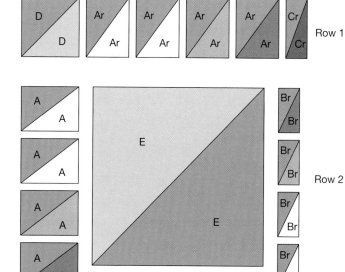

Block assembly

Finishing

1. Sew the two backing strips together and press the seam allowances open.

2. Layer the backing, batting, and quilt top. Quilt by hand or machine, as desired.

3. Sew the binding strips together to form one long strip. Fold the binding in half lengthwise, with wrong sides together, and press. Sew the raw edges of the binding to the edges of the front of the quilt. Turn the folded edge of the binding to the back of the quilt and stitch in place by hand, mitering the corner seams.

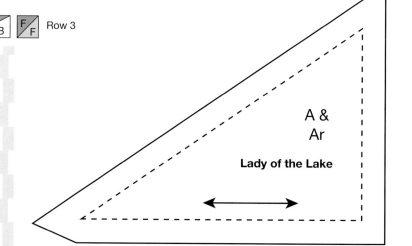

A & Ar

Lady of the Lake

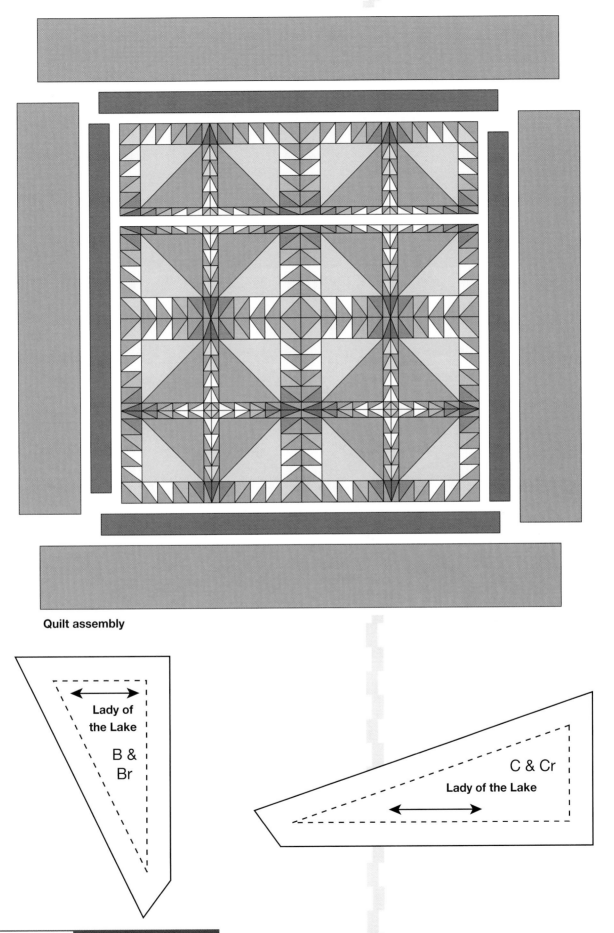

Quilt assembly

Lady of
the Lake

B &
Br

C & Cr

Lady of the Lake

32" x 32"

The paper-pieced blocks in this quilt feature two different color placements. The blocks are alternated and rotated by a quarter-turn to create the quilt design.

Made by the author.

DOUBLE DUTCH

Finished blocks: 12" square

Fabrics and Supplies

Blue	¾ yard
Red	¾ yard
White	1 yard
Red inner border	¼ yard
Blue outer border	½ yard
Backing	1 yard
Batting	36" x 36"
Binding	⅜ yard

Cutting List

Note: Fabric for paper piecing must be cut at least ½" larger than the sections on all sides. Paper-piecing patterns are on pages 85–89.

Off-set Double Dutch block

For Double Dutch Blocks

Fabric	Quantity and pieces to cut
Blue	4 of Section A-1
	2 each: sections A-7 and A-9
	4 of Section B-1
	2 each: sections B-7 and B-9
	4 of Section C-1
	2 of Section C-9
	4 each: sections D-1 and D-9
Red	4 of Section A-4
	2 each: sections A-7 and A-9
	4 of Section B-4
	2 each: sections B-7 and B-9
	4 each: sections C-4 and C-7
	2 of Section C-9
	4 each: sections D-4, D-8, and D-11
White	4 each: sections A-2, A-3, A-5, A-6, A-8, A-10, and A-11
	4 each: sections B-2, B-3, B-5, B-6, B-8, B-10, and B-11
	4 each: sections C-2, C-3, C-5, C-6, C-8, C-10, and C-11
	4 each: sections D-2, D-3, D-5, D-6, D-7, and D-10

Traditional Double Dutch block

For Borders, Backing, and Binding

Fabric	Quantity	Strip width
Red inner border	4 strips	1½"
Blue outer border	4 strips	3½"
Backing	1 square	36" x 36"
Binding	4 strips	desired width

Piecing the Double Dutch Blocks

1. Photocopy the paper-piecing patterns from pages 85–89 onto lightweight paper. You will need four photocopies of each of the four sections of the quilt.

2. Cut the fabrics listed for the pattern sections. Remember to do this from the unmarked side of the paper, with the right side of the fabrics facing up.

3. For each section, place piece #1 on the unmarked side of the paper-piecing pattern with the right side facing up, making sure it covers the entire area of the pattern piece and allows for the seam allowances. Place piece #2 on top of piece #1, right side up, so it covers its pattern piece. Carefully flip piece #2 over onto piece #1, right sides together, making sure that fabric from both pieces covers the sewing line and allows for the seam allowances. Pin the fabric in place. Turn the pattern over, and stitch on the line between pieces #1 and #2.

4. Flip piece #2 over, so that the right side is facing up. Press. Check again to make sure that fabric covers the entire pattern piece.

5. Repeat steps 3 and 4 for the remaining pattern pieces in each paper-pieced section. Refer to the color combination blocks on page 83 as a guide for color placement in each section.

6. When you have completed each section, trim the outside seam allowances to ¼".

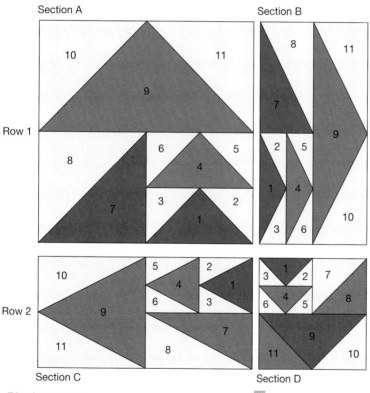

Block assembly

7. Referring to the block assembly diagram, sew the paper-pieced sections in two horizontal rows. Press. Sew the rows together to complete the Double Dutch block. Press. When the blocks are assembled, carefully remove the paper from the back, being careful not to stretch the fabric. Make four Double Dutch blocks, two in each color combination (see page 83).

Assembling the Quilt Center

1. Referring to the quilt assembly diagram, sew the blocks together in two rows of two blocks each. Press.

2. Sew the rows of blocks together. Press the completed quilt center.

Adding the Borders

1. Referring to the quilt assembly diagram, sew two of the 1½"-wide red inner border strips to the top and bottom of the quilt center. Press. Trim the excess fabric even with the edges of the quilt center.

2. Sew the remaining two inner border strips to the sides of the quilt center. Press. Trim the excess fabric even with the edges of the quilt center.

3. Sew two of the 3½"-wide blue outer border strips to the top and bottom of the quilt center. Press. Trim the excess fabric even with the edges of the quilt center.

4. Sew the remaining outer border strips to the sides of the quilt center. Press. Trim the excess fabric even with the edges of the quilt center.

Finishing

1. Layer the backing, batting, and quilt top. Quilt by hand or machine, as desired.

2. Sew the binding strips together to form one long strip. Fold the binding in half lengthwise, with wrong sides together, and press. Sew the raw edges of the binding to the edges of the front of the quilt. Turn the folded edge of the binding to the back of the quilt and stitch in place by hand, mitering the corner seams.

Double Dutch block color combination 1; make 2

Double Dutch block color combination 2; make 2

Quilt assembly

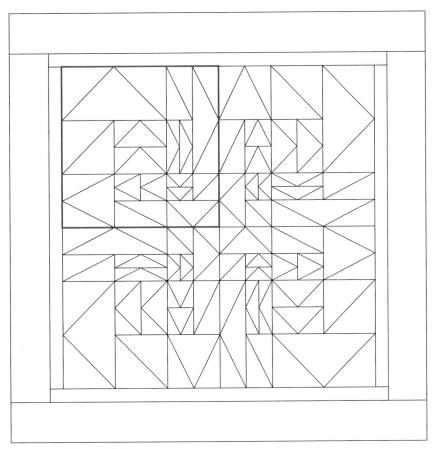

Reproducible quilt drawing

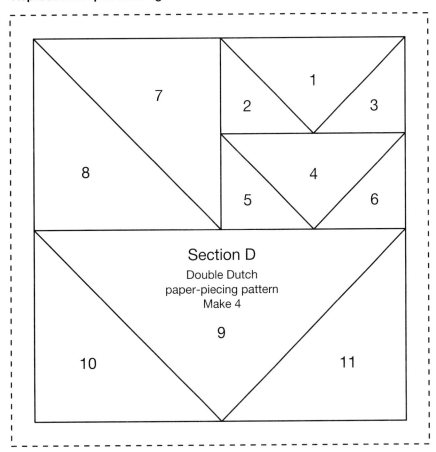

Section D
Double Dutch
paper-piecing pattern
Make 4

Solid lines are seam lines

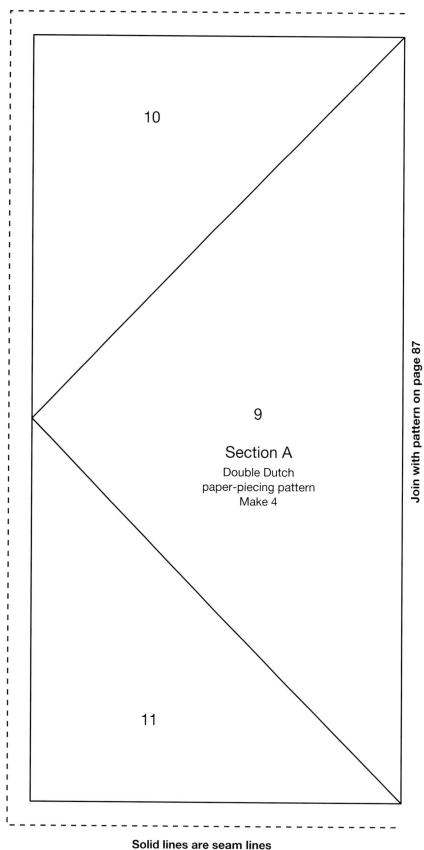

10

9

Section A
Double Dutch
paper-piecing pattern
Make 4

11

Join with pattern on page 87

Solid lines are seam lines

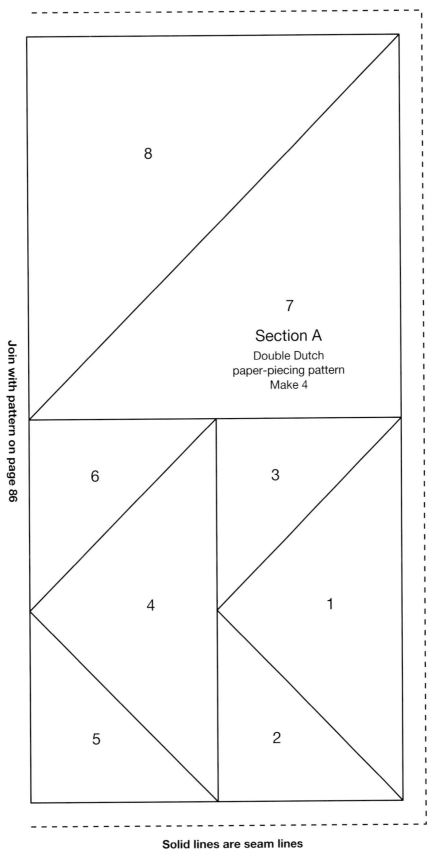

8

7

Section A
Double Dutch
paper-piecing pattern
Make 4

Join with pattern on page 86

6

3

4

1

5

2

Solid lines are seam lines

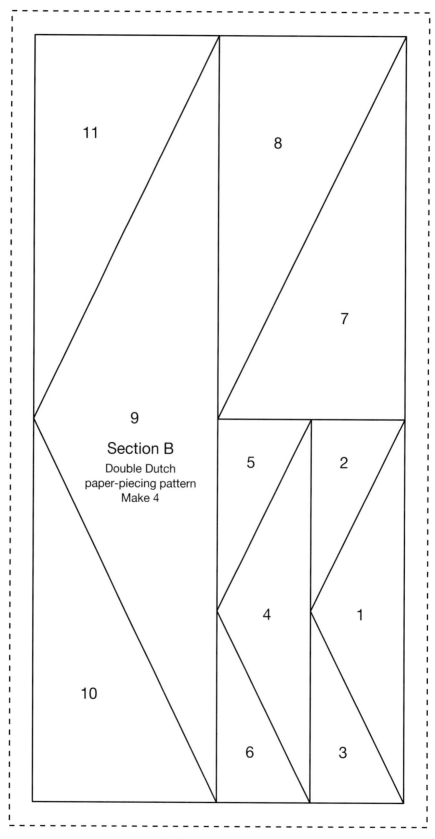

9

Section B
Double Dutch
paper-piecing pattern
Make 4

Solid lines are seam lines

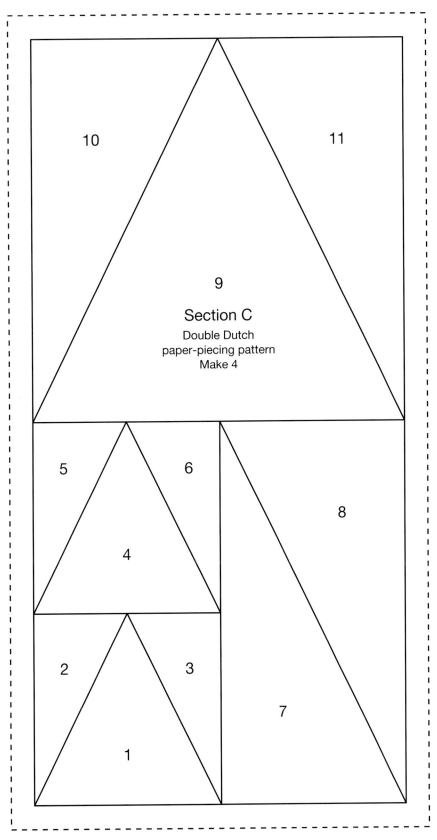

10

11

9

Section C
Double Dutch
paper-piecing pattern
Make 4

5

6

8

4

2

3

7

1

Solid lines are seam lines

46" x 46"

After the block center is shifted off center and redrafted, the blocks in this quilt are rotated by quarter-turns three times to complete the quilt center.

Made by Carol Deal, Bloomington, Illinois.

ONE MORE BLOCK

Finished blocks: 18" square

Fabrics and Supplies

Blue	1 yard
Yellow	1¼ yards
Yellow inner border	¼ yard
Blue outer border	¾ yard
Backing	3 yards
Batting	50" x 50"
Binding	½ yard

Cutting List

Note: Cut all strips across the 42" fabric width.
Pattern pieces A and Ar are on page 93.

For One More Block Blocks

Fabric	Quantity	Strip width	Cut from strips
Blue	1 strip	2⅜"	8 B squares, each 2⅜" x 2⅜"
	4 strips	2¼"	16 A triangles 16 Ar triangles
	2 strips	5"	32 E rectangles, each 5" x 2" 4 F squares, each 5" x 5"
	2 strips	5⅜"	8 C squares, each 5⅜" x 5⅜"
	1 strip	2"	8 D squares, each 2" x 2"
Yellow	1 strip	2⅜"	8 B squares, each 2⅜" x 2⅜"
	4 strips	2¼"	16 A triangles 16 Ar triangles
	3 strips	5"	8 E rectangles, each 5" x 2" 16 F squares, each 5" x 5"
	2 strips	5⅜"	8 C squares, each 5⅜" x 5⅜"
	1 strip	2"	12 D squares, each 2" x 2"

For Borders, Backing, and Binding

Fabric	Quantity	Strip width
Yellow inner border	4 strips	1½"
Blue outer border	5 strips	4½"
Backing	2 strips	25" x 50"
Binding	5 strips	desired width

Off-set One More Block

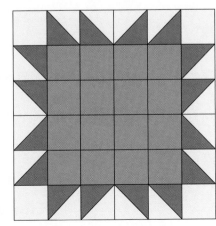

Traditional One More Block

Make 16

Make 16

Make 16

Make 16

Piecing the One More Block Blocks

1. Mark a diagonal line on the wrong side of the 2⅜" yellow B squares. Place a yellow B square and a blue B square right sides together. Sew a ¼" seam on each side of the marked diagonal line. Cut through both fabrics on the diagonal line to make two half-square triangles. Press. Make 16 yellow/blue half-square triangles. The pieced squares should measure 2" x 2".

2. Repeat Step 1 with the eight yellow and blue 5⅜" C squares. The pieced squares should measure 5" x 5".

3. With right sides together, sew the long edge of a blue A triangle to the long edge of a yellow A triangle. Press. Make 16 yellow and blue A/A rectangles.

4. With right sides together, sew the long edge of a blue Ar triangle to the long edge of a yellow Ar triangle. Press. Make 16 Ar/Ar rectangles.

5. Referring to the block assembly diagram, sew the blocks together in six horizontal rows. Press. Sew the rows together. Press. Make four One More Block blocks.

Assembling the Quilt Center

1. Referring to the quilt assembly diagram, sew the blocks together in two rows of two blocks each. Press.

2. Sew rows of blocks together. Press the completed quilt center.

Adding the Borders

1. Referring to the quilt assembly diagram, sew the 1½"-wide yellow inner border strips to the top and bottom of the quilt center. Press. Trim the excess fabric even with the edges of the quilt center.

2. Sew the remaining two inner border strips to the sides of the quilt center. Trim the excess fabric even with the edges of the quilt center.

3. Sew two 4½"-wide blue outer border strips to the top and bottom of the quilt center. Trim the excess fabric even with the edges of the quilt center.

4. Cut one of the remaining outer border strips in half. Sew one of these pieces to the end of a full-length outer border strip to make a longer strip. Repeat with the other full and half outer border strips.

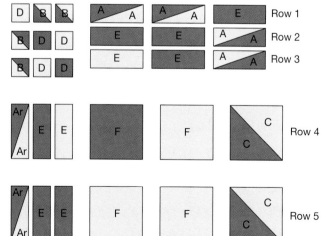

Block assembly

5. Sew the remaining two outer border strips to the sides of the quilt center. Press. Trim the excess fabric even with the edges of the quilt.

Finishing

1. Sew the two backing strips together and press the seam allowances open.

2. Layer the backing, batting, and quilt top. Quilt by hand or machine, as desired.

3. Sew the binding strips together to form one long strip. Fold the binding in half lengthwise, with wrong sides together, and press. Sew the raw edges of the binding to the edges of the front of the quilt. Turn the folded edge of the binding to the back of the quilt and stitch in place by hand, mitering the corner seams.

One More Block

A & Ar

Quilt assembly

48" x 48"

Placing the redrafted Fox and Geese blocks on-point creates the appearance of beautiful flowers in the finished quilt.

Made by Clarise Jefferson, Bloomington, Illinois.

FOX AND GEESE

Finished blocks: 9" square

Fabrics and Supplies

Off-white	⅞ yard
Pink	⅛ yard
Pink print	⅛ yard
Maroon print	½ yard
Dark green	¼ yard
Medium green	½ yard
Maroon purple	⅝ yard
Pink print inner border	¼ yard
Maroon outer border	¾ yard
Backing	3 yards
Batting	52" x 52"
Binding	½ yard

Cutting List

Note: Cut all strips across the 42" fabric width.
Pattern pieces A and Ar are on page 97.

For Fox and Geese Blocks

Fabric	Quantity	Strip width	Pieces to cut
Off-white	1 strip	3⅞"	7 E squares, each 3⅞" x 3⅞", cut in half diagonally
	2 strips	3½"	26 D rectangles, each 2" x 3½"
	4 strips	2¼"	26 A triangles 26 Ar triangles
	2 strips	2⅜"	7 B squares, each 2⅜" x 2⅜" 13 F squares, each 2⅜" x 2⅜", cut in half diagonally
Pink	1 strip	3⅞"	7 C squares, each 3⅞" x 3⅞"
Pink print	1 strip	3⅞"	7 C squares, each 3⅞" x 3⅞"
Maroon print	2 strips	6⅞"	7 G squares, each 6⅞" x 6⅞", cut in half diagonally
Dark green	2 strips	3½"	26 D rectangles, each 2" x 3½"
Medium green	4 strips	2¼"	26 A triangles 26 Ar triangles

Off-set Fox and Geese block

Traditional Fox and Geese block

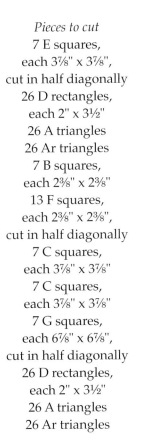

Make 13

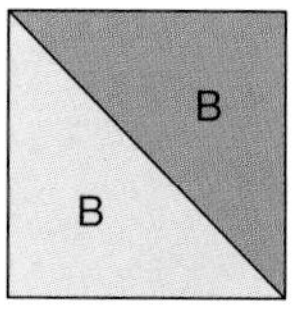

Make 13

Make 26

Make 26

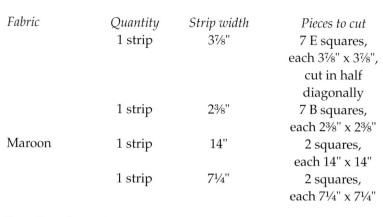

Fabric	Quantity	Strip width	Pieces to cut
	1 strip	3⅞"	7 E squares, each 3⅞" x 3⅞", cut in half diagonally
	1 strip	2⅜"	7 B squares, each 2⅜" x 2⅜"
Maroon	1 strip	14"	2 squares, each 14" x 14"
	1 strip	7¼"	2 squares, each 7¼" x 7¼"

For Borders, Backing, and Binding

Pink print inner border	4 strips	1½"	
Maroon outer border	5 strips	4½"	
Backing	2 strips	26" x 52"	
Binding	5 strips	desired width	

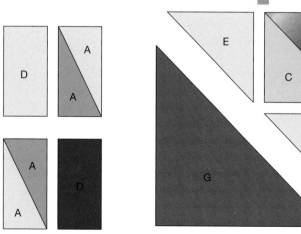

Block assembly

Piecing the Fox and Geese Blocks

1. Mark a diagonal on the wrong side of the 3⅞" pink C squares. Place a pink C square on top of a pink print C square, right sides together. Sew a ¼" seam on each side of the marked diagonal line. Cut through both fabrics on the diagonal line to make two half-square triangles. Press. Make 13 pink/dark purple squares.

2. Repeat Step 1 with the off-white and medium green 2⅜" B squares. Make 13 off-white/medium green squares.

3. With right sides together, sew the long edge of an off-white A triangle to the long edge of a medium green A triangle. Press. Make 26 A/A rectangles.

4. With right sides together, sew the long edge of an off-white Ar triangle to the long edge of a medium green Ar triangle. Press. Make 26 Ar/Ar rectangles.

5. Referring to the block assembly diagram, sew the blocks together in rows. Press. Sew the rows together to complete the blocks. Press. Make 13 Fox and Geese blocks.

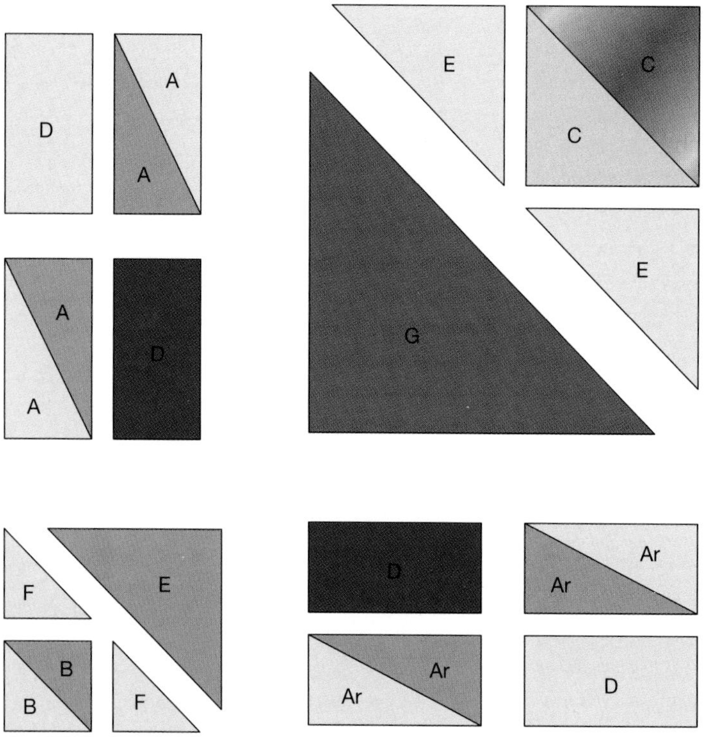

Assembling the Quilt Center

1. Cut the two 14" x 14" maroon squares in quarters diagonally. These eight triangles are the setting squares along the sides of the quilt center.

2. Cut the two 7¼" x 7¼" maroon squares in half diagonally. These four triangles are the corner triangles for the quilt center.

3. Referring to the quilt assembly diagram, arrange the blocks, side setting triangles, and corner triangles in diagonal rows. Press. Sew the diagonal rows together to complete the quilt center. Press.

Adding the Borders

1. Referring to the quilt assembly diagram, sew two of the 1½"-wide pink print inner border strips to the top and bottom of the quilt center. Press. Trim the excess fabric even with the edges of the quilt center.

2. Sew the remaining two inner border strips to the sides of the quilt center. Press. Trim the excess fabric even with the edges of the quilt center.

3. Cut one of the 4½"-wide maroon outer border strips into four equal pieces. Sew one of the pieces to the end of a full-length outer border strip. Repeat with the remaining three outer border strips.

4. Sew two of the outer border strips the top and bottom of the quilt center. Press. Trim the excess fabric even with the edges of the quilt center.

5. Sew the remaining two outer border strips to the sides of the quilt center. Press. Trim the excess fabric even with the edges of the quilt.

Finishing

1. Sew the two backing strips together and press the seam allowances open.

2. Layer the backing, batting, and quilt top. Quilt by hand or machine, as desired.

3. Sew the binding strips together to form one long strip. Fold the binding in half lengthwise, with wrong sides together, and press. Sew the raw edges of the binding to the edges of the front of the quilt. Turn the folded edge of the binding to the back of the quilt and stitch in place by hand, mitering the corner seams.

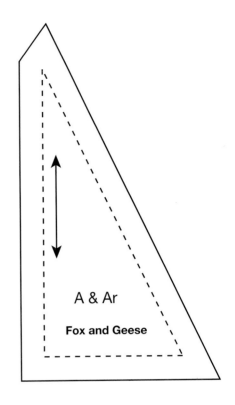

A & Ar

Fox and Geese

Quilt assembly

REPRODUCIBLE QUILT DRAWINGS

You have certainly seen by now that these blocks are very versatile. Changing the color placement or rotating the blocks will give them a different look. Have fun with these designs! Copy the line drawings and get out your biggest box of colored pencils. Play with color placement, make a wild abstract quilt, or see if you find different designs hiding in the quilts. If coloring alone isn't enough for you, copy the drawings and cut the blocks apart on the dark lines which show location of the individual blocks in the quilt. I'm sure you'll have a good time rearranging the blocks for yet another quilt design. Some drawings are included in the project pages – Ohio Star, page 39; Jacob's Ladder, page 45; Sawtooth, page 65; and Double Dutch, page 85. The following pages show line drawings for the rest of the quilts.

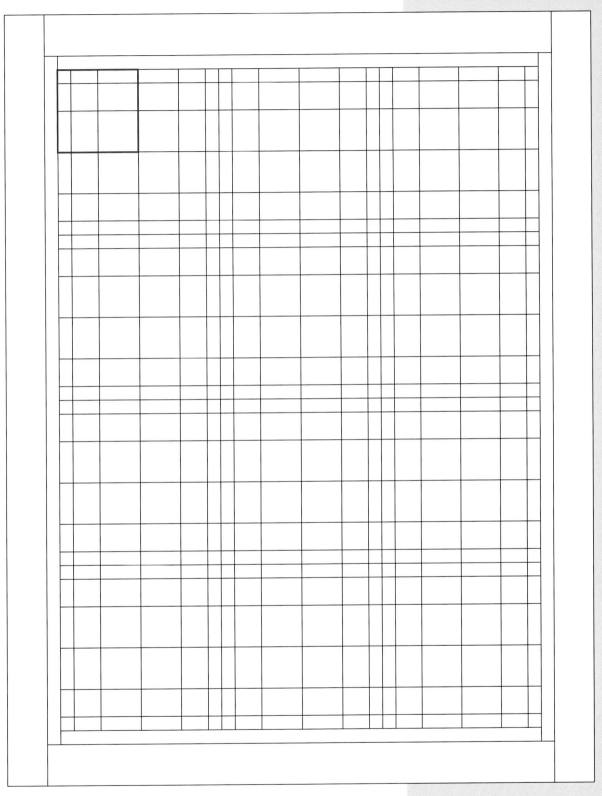

Nine-Patch

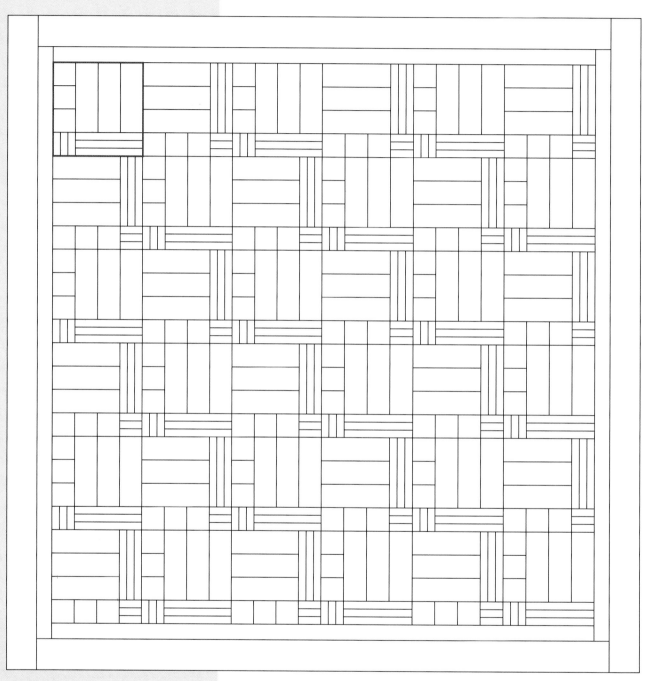

Rail Fence

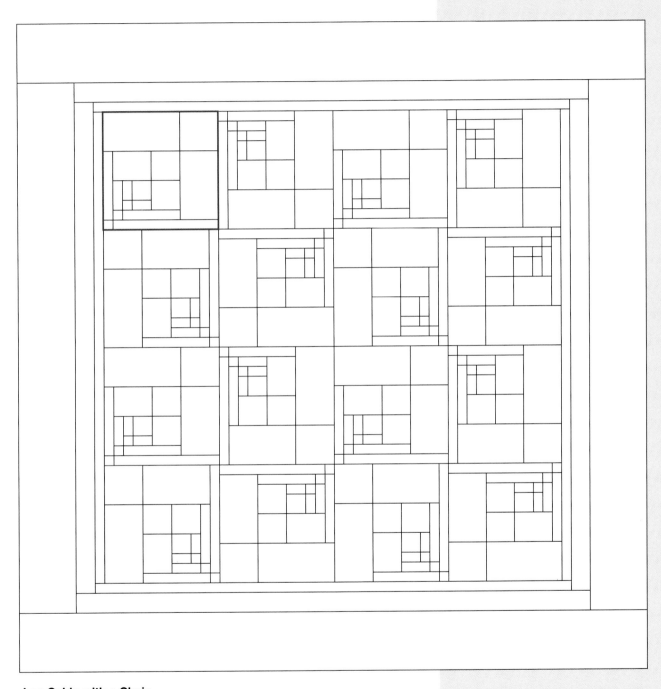

Log Cabin with a Chain

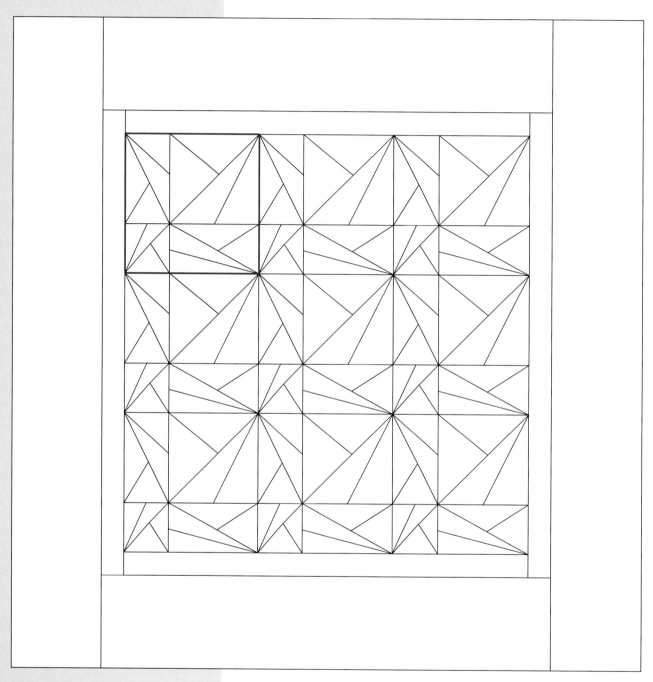

Pinwheel

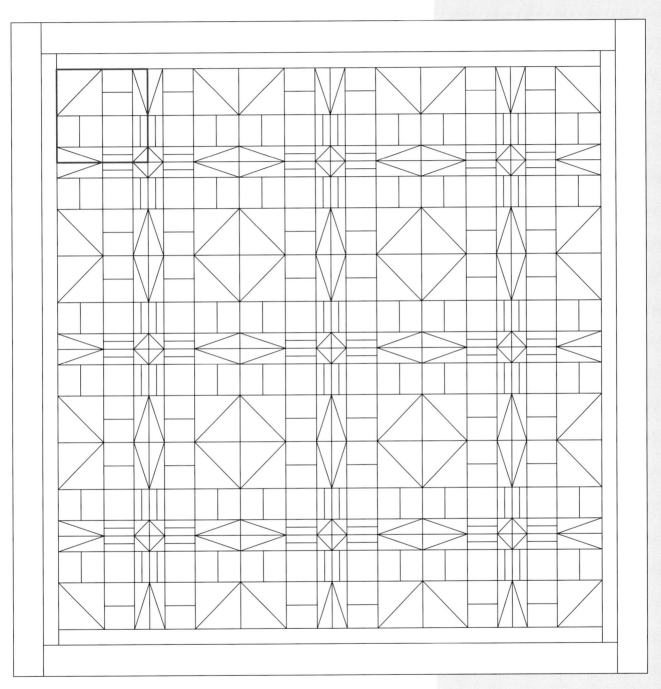

Churn Dash

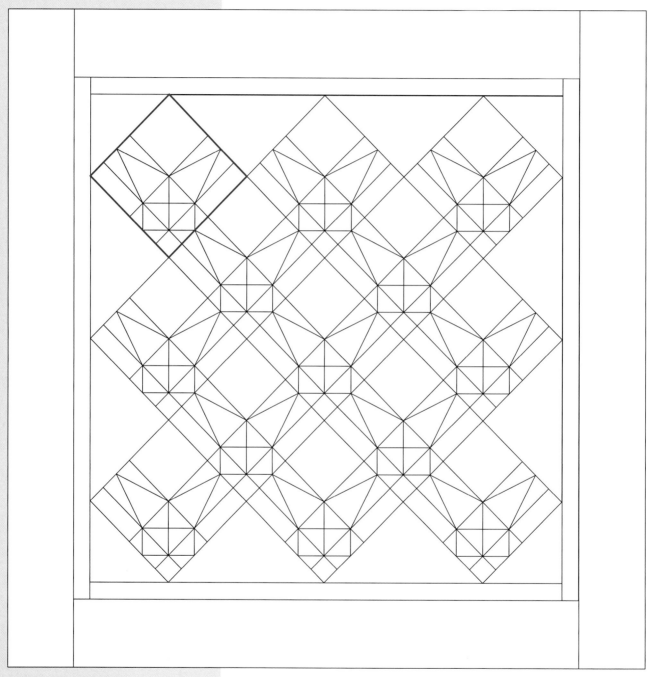

Arkansas Snowflake

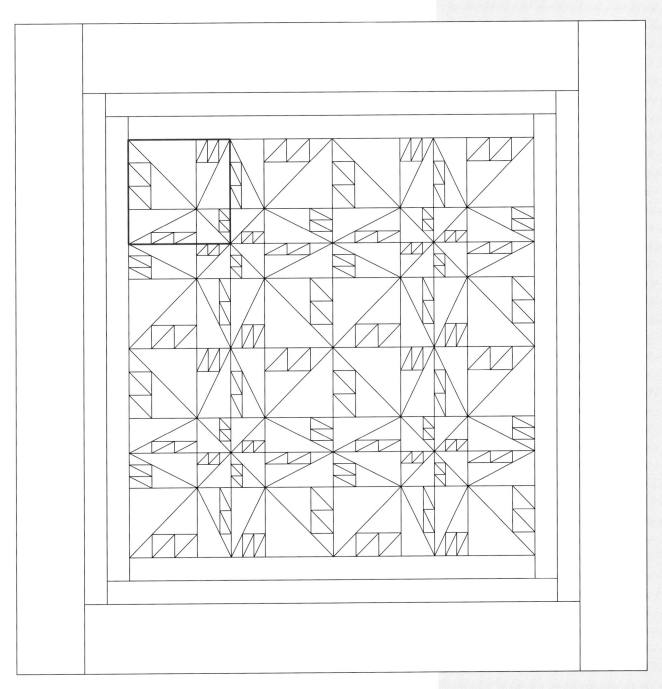

Rosebud

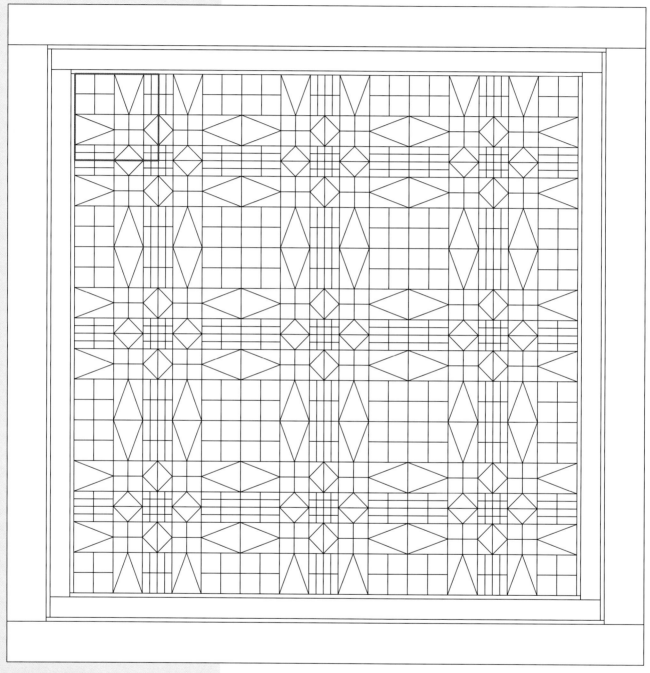

54-40 or Fight

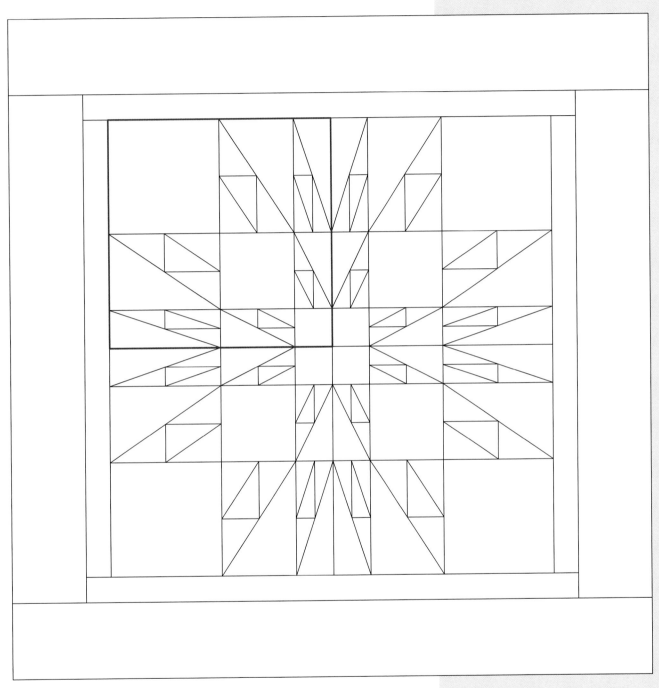

Cat's Cradle

Cheryl A. Adam **OFF CENTER PATCHWORK**

Lady of the Lake

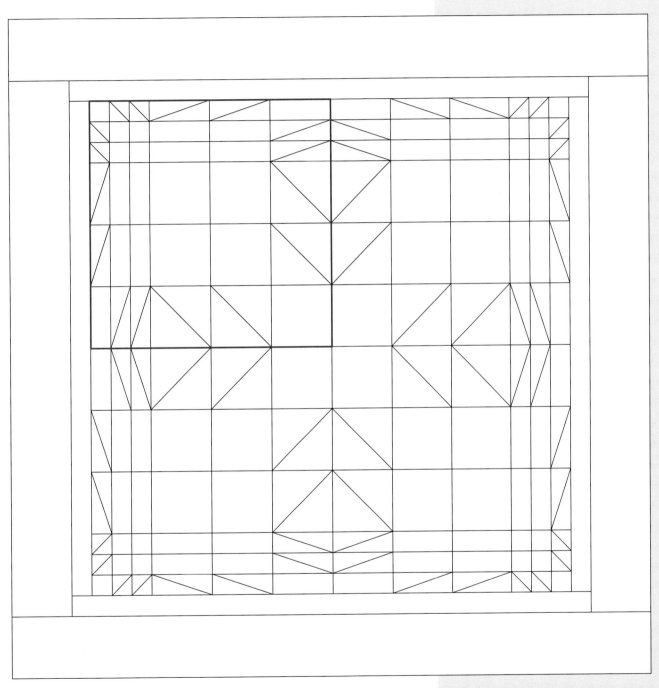

One More Block

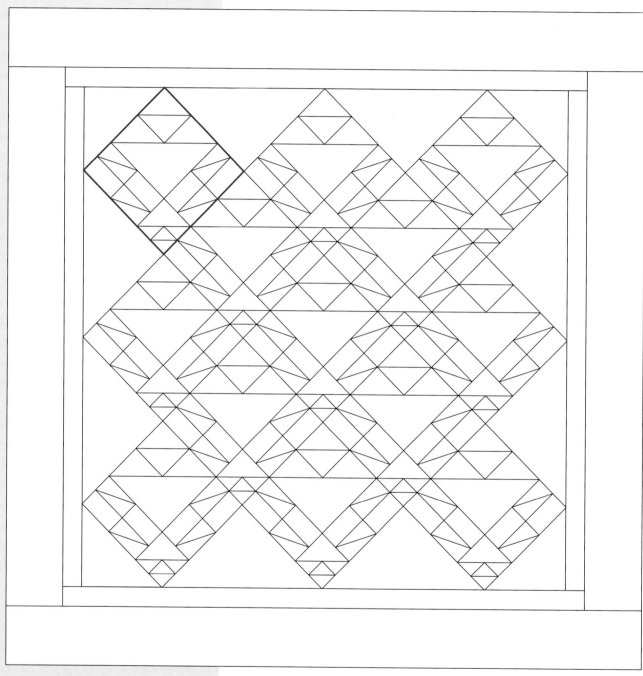

Fox and Geese

ABOUT THE AUTHOR

Trained in architectural engineering, Cheryl started quilting as a hobby in 1982. She turned to quilting as a profession in 1990. Since then she has designed and made quilts for fabric companies and quilting magazines. She enjoys designing quilts and drafting the patterns, which she finds easy because of her educational training. For the past six years, she has taught classes in local quilt shops and guilds.

Cheryl has been published in various advertisements and magazines, including *McCall's Quilting*, *McCall's Quick Quilting*, *Fabric Showcase* magazine, *AQS Address Book* and *Quilt Art Engagement Calendar*, and individual project brochures. She is the technical editor for McCall's Vintage Quilts magazine. Cheryl has exhibited her quilts in numerous shows including ones of local quilt guilds, the Illinois State Fair, the National Quilting Association, Rockome Gardens, and the American Quilter's Society. An active member of the local Hands All Around Quilt Guild and Land of Lincoln State Quilt Guild, she lives in Bloomington, Illinois, with her husband, Bob, and two sons, Martin and Jeff.

OTHER AQS BOOKS

This is only a small selection of the books available from the American Quilter's Society. AQS books are known worldwide for timely topics, clear writing, beautiful color photos, and accurate illustrations and patterns. The following books are available from your local bookseller, quilt shop, or public library.

#6074   us$21.95

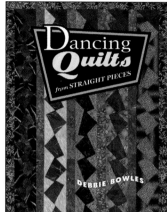

#6210   us$24.95

#5853   us$18.95

#5756   us$19.95

#6212   us$25.95

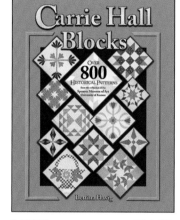

#4957   us$34.95

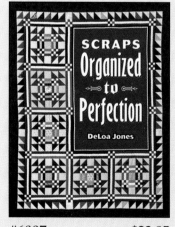

#6007   us$22.95

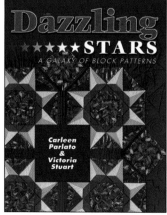

#5844   us$21.95

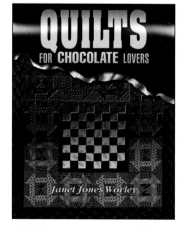

#5758   us$19.95

Look for these books nationally, CALL or VISIT our website at www.AQSquilt.com   **1-800-626-5420**